# Idiot-Syncrasies

## How the Red Sox Were Smart
## Enough to Win the World Series

A. Knoefel Longest

Adams Media
Avon, Massachusetts

Published by
Adams Media, an F+W Publications Company
57 Littlefield Street, Avon, MA 02322 U.S.A
*www.adamsmedia.com*

ISBN: 1-59337-482-8

Printed in the United States of America.

J I H G F E D C B A

**Library of Congress Cataloging-in-Publication Data**
Longest, A. Knoefel.
Idiot-syncrasies / A. Knoefel Longest.
p.  cm.
ISBN 1-59337-482-8
1. Boston Red Sox (Baseball team) 2. Baseball players—United States—Anecdotes. I. Title.

GV875.B62L66 2005
796.357'64'0974461—dc22
2004028600

This publication is designed to provide accurate and authoritative information with regard to the subject matter covered. It is sold with the understanding that the publisher is not engaged in rendering legal, accounting, or other professional advice. If legal advice or other expert assistance is required, the services of a competent professional person should be sought.
—From a *Declaration of Principles* jointly adopted by a Committee of the American Bar Association and a Committee of Publishers and Associations

This book is not authorized or endorsed by Major League Baseball, the Boston Red Sox, or any of its players, past or present. The following are trademarks or service marks of Major League Baseball entities: Major League, Major League Baseball, MLB, the silhouetted batter logo, World Series, National League, American League, Division Series, League Championship Series, All-Star Game, and the names, nicknames, logos, uniform designs, color combinations, and slogans designating the Major League Baseball clubs and entities, and their respective mascots, events and exhibitions.

Interior illustrations by Dennis Cox.

*This book is available at quantity discounts for bulk purchases.*
*For information, please call 1-800-872-5627.*

# Contents

## Part 1 The Lineup / 1

# Part 2 **The Staff / 137**

*for my Mom (for the books)*
*and my Dad (for the baseball)*

## Foreword

# By Jerry Remy

**The Red Sox are World Champions.** That is something every fan who grew up in New England, rooting for the Sox every summer, has wanted to say for a very long time. It is what they have thought about every spring training, and what they hope for throughout every summer, and no matter what happens in the fall, it is usually what they think about most of the winter, too. So many great baseball fans come to Fenway every summer and support the Sox. They follow the team on the road everywhere from Baltimore to Anaheim. And everywhere they go, all summer long, they hope to be able to say those words come October. Every year they hope that this really is the year.

As a former player who spent seven seasons at Fenway, I can tell you that it is also what every player who has ever put on a Sox uniform has wanted to say in October. From the great players of the past like Ted Williams, Dom DiMaggio, Bobby Doerr, and Johnny Pesky, to the guys I played with like Carlton Fisk, Luis Tiant, Fred Lynn, and the great Yaz himself, all the way down to today's players, we have all wanted to be part of the team who made the Red Sox Champions of the World.

For all sorts of reasons, no Red Sox team has quite been able to say those magic words. Until now. Until the 2004 Red Sox became the 2004 World Champion Red Sox. As someone who grew up in New England and has rooted for the Red Sox my entire life, saying those words means as much to me as anyone. But as a former player and now as a broadcaster, I have a deep appreciation of how tough it was to do what this team finally was able to accomplish.

Boston is a great place to play baseball, as good as any in the league. But it is not always an easy place to play. The passion the fans bring to the ballpark works both ways, and just as they will cheer on every great play, they will also let you know when you make a mistake. On top of that, there is the media and all the questions, a lot of them about teams these guys never saw and players they may never have heard of. There is a lot of pressure to be the team who brings home a trophy, and not every player can perform under that kind of pressure.

These guys did. The guys who have been around for awhile now, guys like Trot Nixon and Jason Varitek and Tim Wakefield, learned how to play in Boston a long time ago; and the new guys who have come in, guys like David Ortiz and Kevin Millar and Bill Mueller, have learned fast. More than just play, they seemed to thrive on the energy in the ballpark. Maybe more than any Sox team ever, this team was able to block out all the distractions that come with playing in Boston, and simply play baseball. They enjoyed playing the game and they enjoyed playing with each other as teammates. But this wasn't what made them World Champions. What this did was allow them to play baseball like they were capable of playing it. And with this group that meant playing very well.

In the end, they did all the things they needed to do. They got great starting pitching, they got the hits they needed to get, and they didn't beat themselves. They played hard, as hard when they were down 0-3 to the Yankees as they did when they were up 3-0 to the Cardinals, and they played the game as it was meant to be played. And that's what made them Champions.

After the Sox won the World Series, many Sox fans continued to say that it had not sunk in yet. It didn't seem real yet. Maybe it has by now, but for many they are probably still wondering how it all finally happened. How they came back to beat the Yankees in the ALCS and how they swept the Cardinals in the World Series. We all have some time to think about those questions now. We don't have to worry about that other one anymore, the one about this being the year. We know the answer to that one: 2004. That year was the year the Red Sox became World Champions, and this team was the team that finally got the job done.

# The Eternal Sunshine of Terry Francona

**On the snowy December afternoon** the Red Sox announce Terry Francona as their newest manager—their forty-fourth in club history and second in three years—he sits upright in Fenway Park with his arms folded in front of him, leaning slightly forward toward a microphone, and smiles as he faces a pressroom full of reporters and cameras. Head and chin both clean-shaven and reflecting camera lights, the features of his face—the prominent nose, the smooth, teardrop chin, the smallish eyes behind a pair of thin, silver-framed glasses—shift and reshift with respect to the wide centerpiece of a smile.

# Winter

Francona's smile is a natural, bright, effortless one; his full cheeks pushing up to make the smallish eyes even smaller, the smile-lines deep and clear, sliding around the mouth and down the forward chin. He flashes it between each question, between each sentence, seemingly between each of his exuberant words. And not without reason. At forty-five, and with only four seasons of experience as a major league manager (and all of them losing seasons), Terry Francona has just been named to one of the highest-profile managerial positions in all of baseball at a time when the profile of both manager and team are nearing all-time highs.

He is the new manager of the Boston Red Sox Baseball Club, one of the glory titles in baseball. It is the lead on-field presence of a proud and legendary baseball tradition, housed in an antique gem of a ballpark, followed throughout New England and across the country by a nation of religiously devoted fans, and, as Francona now sees, the constant, dedicated subject of a rather large and (as Francona will soon see) rather intense press corps.

It is not, however, a position without a few significant, and fairly peculiar, catches; among them the fact that the majority of Francona's forty-three predecessors have departed quickly and under rather unpleasant terms (left, that is, without smiles on their faces), including his immediate predecessor, who happened to be one of the more successful men to hold the position. And then, of course, there is the simple, daunting reality of the expectations inherent in the job description: Achieve what no one in your position has achieved in eighty-six years, and achieve it right now.

Francona seems to understand all this in an academic, sterile kind of way as he articulates this awareness in his clear, energetic statements. He says all the right things, and he says them all with a smile. He is *glad to be here*. He is *looking forward to meeting the guys*. He is *excited about the opportunity*, and he is ready *to work hard to get the job done*. He is *enthusiastic*, he is *confident*, and above all else, he is (as a cringe of familiarity ripples through the pressroom): *optimistic*.

## Spring

Three months later, when the Red Sox open spring training in Fort Myers, Francona stands with his arms crossed on a sunny patch of grass behind home plate, facing a loose crescent of reporters in shirtsleeves and sunglasses, and smiles. The winter months since his introduction have—through a series of successful acquisitions and one significantly unsuccessful acquisition—heightened both the profile of his position and its already substantial expectations. Not only is he expected to achieve what no other in his position has achieved in eighty-six years, it is now generally accepted that he has the team to do so. Therefore, failure to achieve this level of success will be generally accepted as his fault alone.

But, as he smiles and tells the reporters, he is *excited about the way this team is put together.* He likes *the flexibility it offers him as a manager.* He thinks *they will be very tough to beat this season*; and he is, still, very *optimistic*. He smiles and says these things, all the right things, beneath the bill of a crisp blue Red Sox hat, his eyes bright, his voice energetic and pointed, and the clear, clean lines around his mouth arching smoothly down to his clean-shaven chin.

He is attentive but relaxed, posture upright but with an easy tilt of the head as he answers the next question, smiles, says all the right things. The reporters nod and smile, and from behind home plate a soft ripple of laughter is heard in the warm, early morning sunshine.

## Early Summer

Three months later, with the Sox taking the field at Fenway in the middle innings of a close, late-May game against Toronto, Francona sits by himself at the far right end of the Sox dugout, relentlessly working a large clump of chaw in the side of his jaw. He sits with both hands pressed to the bench beneath him, elbows locked and shoulders leaned over his knees and rocking forward to a quick, nervous rhythm. The young season had started off well enough—the Sox jumping out to an early division lead, carried by the strength of solid starting pitching and near-perfect bullpen work. But they have since lost their way a bit, and have begun to play a muddling, maddening brand of baseball that has kept them bobbing a half game up or a half game behind for nearly two weeks.

Francona has acknowledged as much in his postgame interviews, but he feels *the team is starting to come together.* He feels that *the team knows what it needs to do,* that they just need *to execute better.* He *likes what he has seen in the last few days* though, and is still, as ever, *optimistic.* He is, however, no longer smiling. Instead, as the inning begins, he removes the wad of chaw and twists open a bottle of water, takes two quick drinks and spits them out in two long streams, then pulls out a new pouch and packs his jaw full of pink gum. He sits back down, plants his hands on the bench, and begins to rock back and forth. As he works the gum (a massive, painful-looking protrusion on the side of his mouth), we notice a shadow across his jaw and chin, and a small, shallow crease between his eyebrows we had not noticed before. The eyes are still bright, still attentive and energetic, but are perhaps framed a bit more by the tiny and now-visible lines beneath them, and he looks distinctly like a man who might benefit from a few more hours of sleep.

## Late Summer

Three months later, with the Sox tossing uniforms and cleats aside in the Fenway clubhouse behind him, Francona stands in a small antechamber to the side and faces one reporter and one camera. Beneath its one light, he says, in a raspy, tired voice, that he *really thinks things are starting to come together.* His eyes, as he says these words, are deep-set and rimmed by dark, prominent circles; the cheeks below them clammy and pale; the lines around the mouth now sharp; the chin and jaw covered with a growth of stubble. He looks at the reporter, says he feels like *we're just not doing the things you have to do to win baseball games;* but that he feels like *we're almost there,* and that *the bottom line is we just need to execute.*

These comments come despite the fact that the Sox have played the same muddling, frustratingly inconsistent brand of .500 baseball for the better part of three months. They have just lost a miserable, damp, and drizzly grinder of a game to the White Sox, and now stand at exactly 10½ games behind the first-place Yankees. Francona, however, is still *optimistic*—despite his raspy, tired voice; despite his dark, bloodshot eyes; despite his blanched complexion, stubbled jaw, and the tired, suddenly very old-looking slope of his neck. Despite all this, he thinks *we are really close to putting it all together.*

It is these types of statements (all the wrong words at all the wrong times), along with the nervous and ritualistic chaw-water-gum routine and the incessant rocking on the bench, that have become so familiar over the summer that give these weary, raspy-voiced statements of optimism a slightly troubling ring. They seem forced, searching, and vaguely delusional. Francona, no longer trying to attempt a smile as the interview wraps and the light turns off, looks utterly exhausted, utterly spent, and very much like a man who might soon need medical (if not clinical) attention.

# Autumn

Three months later, with the Sox down 3-0 to the Yankees in the ALCS and dressing for Game Four in the clubhouse beyond, Francona sits behind the desk of his clubhouse office and looks down at a wide, blank card. He has just returned from facing a pressroom filled with both national and international baseball press corps, whom he has told he is *still looking at this as just one game.* He is still confident in this team. He still thinks *all we need to do is focus on today's game,* and that they *can't worry about what happened last night.* He thinks his team will *lay it all on the line tonight.*

He did not smile when he made these statements, and his tired eyes were calm and distant, his voice energetic but worn, forcing words and phrases out in a rapid succession of baseball clichés and axioms, scraping. He looked thin behind the microphone, his elbows holding him up rather than resting in front of him. He gave the general impression of a desperate man nearing the desperate end of a long, troubling nightmare of a season.

And yet, as he sits in his office now, his team loosely assembling in the clubhouse outside his door, he does not feel desperation. He is surely tired (has not slept much or slept well in months), and he is weary of the crush of reporters and cameras and microphones that have filled much of his immediate personal space over the last six months. But, regardless of his physical state, he is, still: *optimistic.* Confident, even.

Where does this deep, silent well of eternal optimism—the same optimism he felt in December, in May, in August, and now in October—come from? What inner reserves of mental resilience does he now call on to convince himself, and to try and convince others, that the situation is not nearly as desperate as it seems? Where does he find the strength? What delusional dreams or psychotic fantasies does he spin for himself to justify such blind optimism? Where does it all come from, what does it all come back to?

It has, it turns out, been in front of him all along. On the cusp of one of the most devastating disappointments in the history of a club known for its devastating disappointments—and with the very real possibility of being held personally responsible for this disappointment by millions of fans, a small battalion of media, and, perhaps, even his own employers—Francona spreads his left hand out flat over the source of his confidence, over the magic card with the MLB logo that lays blank before him.

He looks down at it, picks up a pen, and, starting in the top left column and moving top to bottom, begins to write:

Damon, cf
Cabrera, ss
Ramirez, lf
Ortiz, dh
Varitek, c
Nixon, rf
Millar, 1b
Mueller, 3b
Bellhorn, 2b

Below this, he writes in the name of his starting pitcher: Lowe. He then moves down the card and fills in his bench: Kapler, Roberts, Reese, Mientkiewicz. Then, the bullpen: Timlin, Embree, Leskanic, Myers, Mendoza, Arroyo, Wakefield, Foulke.

We imagine him there, looking down this list (thinking quickly of the two Hall of Fame names not listed, Schilling and Martinez) and looking over its familiar names. A lifetime in baseball has taught Terry Francona how to decipher meaning from such lists, just as nearly a year of studious observation has taught him the meanings and suggestions inherent within the one he looks at now. He knows what each of these names is capable of doing on a baseball diamond, and seeing them all there in a row, he knows what they are capable of as a group. He knew something of this even way back in December, on the day he was hired, knew a bit more in spring and a great deal more in early summer, and by late summer had grown somewhat desperate to see that potential finally reached.

But here, on the 17th of October, 2004, with his team one loss away from winter, Terry Francona can still look over this group of names and feel confident, optimistic even, in their capability to win any baseball game, against any opponent, at any time—no matter the circumstances. Bolstered by this knowledge (as true now as ever), he sketches his signature across its bottom line, sets his pen down, blinks his weary eyes over his roster and lineup, over his team, and smiles.

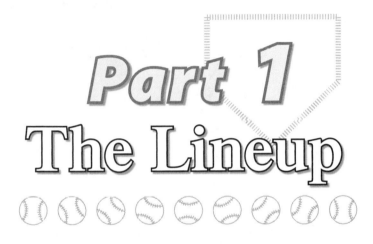

# Part 1
# The Lineup

# Johnny Damon, Superstar

**Johnny Damon** looks, acts, and plays baseball like a rock star; and although it is only the last of these three that made him a key player in the Red Sox' championship season, it is the combination of all three that has made him so beloved among Red Sox fans. And it all started, as it often does with rock stars, with the hair.

# First Impressions

Slightly shaggy, slightly stubbled, Damon walked off the field in Yankee Stadium in mid-October 2003 as a popular and important figure among his Red Sox teammates and fans. He was a solid-hitting (although traditionally slow-starting) leadoff man with speed both on the bases and in center field. The Sox relied heavily on Damon and often their success could be gauged as a reflection of his own, and during his first two seasons in Boston, he more or less provided what was asked of him. He hit a few big home runs. He made a few spectacular catches against the Fenway walls. He was a .280 hitter, which was good but, well, *just* good.

Off the field, the clean-shaven guy from Kansas (who grew up and now lives in Florida) had his own fan club, his own Web site, and his own niche of sincerely devoted, highly enthusiastic, and (by all accounts) predominantly female following among the larger citizenry of Red Sox fans. So as he walked off the baseball stage for the last time in 2003, Johnny Damon was generally known as, *you know, a good ballplayer, a good guy to have on the team, plays hard and gets the job done most of the time, and sort of awkward looking but, you know, popular with the ladies.* And that was it.

Five months later, on a sunny afternoon in Fort Myers, he stepped back onto the 2004 stage like a rock star—long hair, full beard, shades, stepping out of a slick blue sports car with a flashy blonde on his arm—nailing the look on his very first day. Of course, he had the Porsche in 2003, and the flashy blonde (then his girlfriend, now his wife), and we can assume the shades as well; but not the hair, and not the beard. While great hair alone does not necessarily turn a mild star into a superstar, it certainly is a step in the right direction. And, significantly, it gives story-starved journalists something to write about and take pictures of during the long, drawn-out month of March.

# MONSTER minutiae

Some credit deserves to be given to the Red Sox GM (and owner John Henry as well). While other teams in other cities see fit to preside over their club's grooming habits like a father over children in his house, the Red Sox have chosen to treat the men on their roster like men, and let them worry about their own hair. Some Sox players concerned themselves with their hair (Damon, Pedro, Millar) and some did not (Mueller, Nixon, the entire Red Sox bullpen), and since neither seems to have much to do with baseball, the Red Sox Baseball Operations office has left the trimming and grooming of its team to their respective barbers, and focused instead on building a championship team. (And, by the way, it worked.)

The hair—brown and shoulder-length at the time, with a trim brown beard—was new and different, an amusing and entertaining subject compared to the heavier, more dire topics echoing from Fort Myers, and from day one of spring training the hair was *the* Johnny Damon story. When asked how it came about, Damon said he had grown it out during other offseasons, that it was comfortable and he liked it, but that he had always shaved before spring training; this year, he decided to keep it. When kidded about his resemblance to Jesus, Damon laughed. When asked if he planned to keep it during the season, Damon said yes (and added that Theo said he could), and did. The hair stayed throughout spring training, growing out to lay across his shoulders on Opening Day, the beard even thicker and more impressive, and it stayed on into the warm afternoons of May, by which time both Johnny and the hair (although at times not in that order) had developed something of a following. Johnny Damon, the popular guy with a primarily female fan club, suddenly had disciples—an entire group of young men and women wearing T-shirts with his face on them and donning tributary wigs and fake beards, all congregating in the centerfield bleachers and mock bowing to the mock prophet himself.

To his credit, Damon not only acknowledged his new following, but encouraged it, answering reporters that yes, he had seen them, and yes, it was nice to be paid homage in such a way, and yes, he wanted to thank them for coming out (and, later, for traveling to road games as well). But the disciples in center were only the most visible evidence of a much wider phenomenon as the subject of Damon's new look broadened beyond the Red Sox circle. Non–Sox fans, non–baseball fans even, looked in and observed and discussed, and then almost inevitably asked their Red Sox acquaintances one of the more popular questions of the spring—*Hey, what's up with Johnny Damon's hair?* T-shirts were printed; more and better wigs (and by better, we mean worse) appeared in the stands at Fenway; a billboard of his face went up a block from the ballpark; and when Gillette made a donation to the charity of his choice in exchange for shaving his beard, and this public shaving drew 2,500 people into Copley Square in the middle of the afternoon on a weekday, it became official—the man with the rock star hair had achieved rock star status.

# How to Hit Like a Rock Star

None of this, however, helped Damon do his job or helped the Red Sox win games as much as what he did when his famous hair was tucked under a blue helmet, or flowing from beneath a blue hat as he sprinted across the outfield, and none of this helped make history as much as the one quick swing in October, in Game Seven of the 2004 ALCS, back once again in Yankee Stadium. In the second inning, with Cabrera on first, Mueller on second, and Millar on third, Johnny Damon steps to the plate desperately needing to make something happen. Through the first six games of the series, he has suffered through one of the worst (and most poorly timed) slumps of his career, has failed to score runs, has failed to get on base for the opportunity to score runs.

Now, with one out, he steps into the box with his left foot first and his right stretched far outside, his shoulders almost square to the mound as he holds the bat upright away from his chest, facing new Yankee pitcher Javier Vasquez. The hair, fanning out from the back and sides of his dark helmet, hangs down past his shoulders now, and the beard is full but neatly trimmed, red turtleneck collar running up beneath it. His long red sleeves stretch down to black Franklin batting gloves as Vasquez now comes set and Damon swings the bat around once and pulls the right foot into the box, still open. He bobs off the front foot, bat bouncing at his back shoulder. Just as the Yankee Stadium crowd settles back in and Red Sox fans turn back to their screens for the first pitch Vasquez delivers, the ball hangs out over the inside half of the plate, and Damon takes one quick swing—driving the ball high and deep into the right field bleachers. In an instant, all his outs are forgiven and all his struggles forgotten as he jogs a historic lap around the bases and high-fives his teammates at home, and on his way back to the dugout, pulls off his helmet and shakes his long hair out like a rock star.

## How to Run Like a Rock Star

It is this swing that will always be mentioned whenever old baseball fans mention Johnny Damon, but the image that will perhaps be more vividly remembered will not be that of a jog, but a sprint. The more typical Johnny Damon highlight involves him digging through second and bursting around third, on his way home, with Fenway on its feet and leaning toward the plate. It is the Johnny Damon moment, and there are many of them. None, however, is more classic in form or dramatic in pace than the final play of a Thursday night game against the A's in July—the definitive Johnny Damon moment tucked nicely within the definitive Johnny Damon weekend.

Sox fans need only a glance back to that night to see him standing there, fists held before him as he crouches off first, looking in as Bill Mueller takes his stance at the plate. In the bottom of the tenth and with one out, Damon's first-pitch single has sent a ripple of applause through Fenway. Now, with Mueller up and the game tied, the Sox stand a base hit away from moving the winning run into scoring position. The hit comes on a 1-0 pitch, as A's pitcher Jim Lehr delivers a fastball low and away and Mueller reaches down and whips it out into the gap in left-center. Damon takes off on contact, bursting toward second as the ball bounces once and rolls toward the track and he digs hard through second and, just then, the ball takes quick hop into the midsection of A's outfielder Mark Kotsay and Damon drops his head and sprints hard through third—Fenway on its feet now and roaring—and charges home as his hair flies back off his shoulders, hard down the line as the roar builds to a crescendo and he barrels in and dives and crashes down across home plate in a cloud of dirt and hair. With the catcher's glove still pressed to his hip, Damon looks up through the dust to umpire Bill Miller, who kneels over him with arms spread wide, palms out—safe all the way.

## How to Field Like a Rock Star

There are other images, of course, hundreds—images of Damon sprinting across the outfield, crashing into the scoreboard wall (hat popping off, hair flying); sprinting from first to second and diving in ahead of a catcher's throw (likewise); sliding in on a low liner to sweep the ball off the centerfield grass at the last instant—but all of these examples have one element in common. It is an element that is not much valued by statisticians but is savored dearly by fans, and which is often called a flair for the dramatic, but is more accurately and simply defined as style. Johnny Damon, the baseball player on the baseball diamond, has it; and it has nothing to do with hair.

The home run in the ALCS was not just a home run; it was a grand slam; and not just a grand slam in the ALCS but a grand slam in Game Seven of the ALCS. Similarly, his only home run in the World Series was not just a home run in the World Series but a leadoff home run, in the final game. He hit only two postseason home runs, and both provided the winning runs in deciding games. That's style. His mad dashes around the bases do not often end in a clean pop-up slide, but a furious head-first, helmet-dispensing dive, and this, too, is style. His running catches in the outfield do not often end with a graceful glide in the air and soft sweep of the glove, but instead a bone-shaking, hat-disposing clatter against a steel wall; body, glove, and hat all landing in a pile of dirt on the warning track; and this also is a kind of style. Some would say this is instead a kind of awkwardness, a lack of body control and a lack of grace, but this misses the point—it is not the merit of the play, but the manner in which it is made. And although baseball scouts and general managers and statisticians concern themselves with the former, the latter is of at least equal if not greater interest to fans of the game.

## RED SOX NATION

There have been others who have played center field for the Sox with a bit of style, chief among them Fred Lynn (1974–1980), whose diving catches across the grass and leaping crashes into the wall are the standard by which many great Fenway catches have been measured. In fact, Damon and others owe a particular debt to Lynn, who at one point crashed so hard into the then-bare steel centerfield wall that it prompted owner Tom Yawkey to install padding across certain sections of the outfield.

There are any number of ways to make a catch of great baseball merit. The elegantly timed and smooth, fluid sail of a more refined breed of outfielder (say, a Torii Hunter or a Jim Edmonds) is truly fascinating to watch, and we observe it with a kind of awe and appreciation, and give a breathless *wow*, and the proper respectful applause. It is a classical performance, and we appreciate it as such. It does not, however, rock.

What *does* rock is Johnny Damon disregarding the warning of the warning track and charging shoulder- and head-first into a steel wall and landing in a dirty pile, shaking his head. What rocks is Johnny Damon diving through home with the game-winning run and popping up with his bill tipped forward and immediately grabbing his helmet and spiking it in the dirt behind him as he throws his arms around Ortiz. While we all can appreciate the gentlemanly tip of the cap, it simply does not rock like Johnny Damon sprinting out to center field and giving his adoring, bowing disciples a strong, solid double-point as they shout out from the bleachers to him, *You rock, Johnny!*

## How to Live Like a Rock Star

The same enthusiastic double-point turns into a wave later on, on an off day, when the baseball rock star slips on his shades and cruises down Mass Ave. as a stylish celebrity on his way to an appearance. Fans and followers on the sidewalks, recognizing what is possibly the most recognizable head in New England behind the wheel of a sleek convertible, call out to him and wave and he, slowing, returns their wave and smiles. At the appearance (a department store promotion), he smiles again, and stands in for a series of pictures, his arm around a nearly delirious young fan.

When it is over, he gives an interview to a local television crew, signs a parade of autographs, and answers questions from a journalist. He then stands and smiles and puts his arm around one more fan for one more picture, and one more after that, signs another round of autographs, and finally slips his shades back on and pulls away, smiling and giving a quick wave from the convertible; then, quickly stopping, he signs one more autograph over the side of his door, hands it up, and waves as he pulls away. It is Johnny Damon's rock star life—one we recognize from all the usual American by-products of fame (the attention, the spotlight, the money). But something is different here, in this scene and with this rock star. It is subtle but present nonetheless, and our first hint of this comes from listening to him in front of the television cameras.

## How to Stand in the Spotlight
## Like a Rock Star

Damon gives hundreds of interviews throughout the season, thousands even, to television, radio, and newspaper reporters; before the game, during batting practice, after the game, in the hotel, and at every appearance. He is asked questions and answers them thoughtfully and thoroughly, more so perhaps than any other member of the team. He talks by choice, a great deal of time each and every day. It is only when we learn that Johnny Damon was afflicted with a severe speech impediment as a child—which he worked tirelessly on for years to overcome—that this choice begins to take on its full weight. Many fans and followers might not be aware of this history, but then, that is only because Damon himself has never seen reason to make much of it. He has mentioned it at times, casually, and when pressed has said little more than that it took a great deal of work to defeat. But this is more than enough for us to understand its significance, which is that all the interviews, and all the appearances, and all the questions, do not come naturally for Johnny Damon.

He was not, as they say, born a star. And he does not cultivate his fame as a born star often does, by stepping into the light only to bask under it, by speaking only to hear how lovely one's own voice is, and only to take credit for the work one has already been substantially credited for. Instead, Damon does almost the exact opposite with his fame. When asked about his own performance, his most common tone is self-deprecation, and his most common instinct is to point out to others his lack of gracefulness in the field, to laugh at the awkwardness of his slide, to remind others of the massive slump that preceded the heroic home run.

## How to Give Back Like a Rock Star

In his most famous comments of all, which came on the cusp of the 2004 playoffs, he questions his own and his teammates' intelligence. These are hardly the remarks of a man who would naturally seek the spotlight, and rather seem like the words of a man whom the spotlight has found. Why then does he remain so fixed beneath it? Again we listen to him speak, and hear him mention the fans, and we remember the playful double-point into the bleachers, the wave from the convertible, and the extra round of autographs at the appearance, and the patient, smiling pictures, and the fan club that he supports and whose annual meeting he attends, and we begin to see that Johnny Damon is doing exactly what so many celebrities give lip service to but so few back up with their actions: He is giving back the attention he has received.

The waves, the interviews, the appearances, the photos, the autographs—they all acknowledge the tremendous outpouring of attention that has been showered down upon Johnny Damon throughout his career and particularly during this season. He does not point into the crowd and acknowledge every worshiping call to him from the centerfield bleachers because he has to, and he does not sign autographs or give photo-ops because it is part of his job, and he does not speak to the media on a daily basis and give long interviews because it is what comes naturally to him or because he is the best speaker on the team (although he is quite funny and much more insightful than he gives himself credit for). He does it all, it seems, because these are exactly what his fans want him to do—hear him speak, see him acknowledge their cheers in the bleachers, have their pictures taken with him, and have his autograph.

Does he enjoy the attention and the praise and the money? Absolutely. He loves it, but this is exactly the point. Damon, unlike so many others in his profession and of his status, seems to embrace and enjoy the flattery and luxury of his status exactly as much as we imagine someone in his profession would. More importantly, his actions have shown that he appreciates it all and takes none of it for granted. And this is what has made him a superstar—because the attention he gives reflects back upon him, magnified by its senders. It is performance and style on the field that made him a star to begin with, and it was the look that made him famous, but it is his willingness to accept this status and fame, and his willingness to make himself accessible that has ultimately magnified Johnny Damon into his current, rock star status.

**idiot RULE:** *It is a simple game: You catch the ball, you throw the ball, you hit the ball (but it always helps to have good hair).*

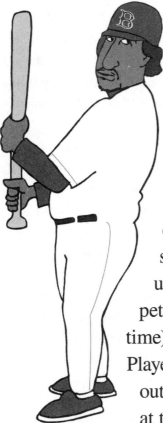

# Chapter 2

# Destination: Mannyland

**It is the single greatest honor** an individual may receive within the game. More so even than the MVP of the league, which represents performance over the expanded, expansive stretch of a season, and more so than individual records that are so often a competition against the game itself (and time), the award for Most Valuable Player in the World Series represents outstanding individual achievement at the highest level of competition in the game, and is, therefore, a measure of greatness. To receive it is a solemn, sacred honor.

# Welcome to Mannyland

The Commissioner of Baseball, Bud Selig, seems to understand this significance as he stands in the visitor's clubhouse in St. Louis, holding the MVP trophy moments after the Red Sox have won the World Series. He seems to be trying to convey this understanding across the stage to the man with the spastic hair and wide, full grin, who stands across from him wearing a damp gray championship T-shirt and looking out into the celebrating clubhouse around him. He is Manny Ramirez—the MVP of the World Series.

"The Most Valuable Player award," Selig begins, "in the historic 2004 World Series goes to Manny"—(Manny catches the glance of a teammate and gives a gleeful double-point and smile).

"Manny, it was a tremendous performance," Selig goes on, "I congratulate you, and"—(again Manny's eyes wander off the platform and spot a friend; he double-points away from the presentation and smiles). Selig hands the large, silver spire of a trophy across to Manny, who takes it and cups it to his side as the commissioner steps away and a television reporter steps in to interview the MVP.

She asks him about unfinished business. He says he was confident, that he believed in himself. Then he is asked if he believes in curses, and in one of those rare moments in sports when an obvious, standard-issue baseball cliché is intended, but through a slight muddle is delivered with greater meaning and deeper significance than even its speaker perhaps intended, Manny answers, "I don't believe in curses. I think you make your own destination."

It is an innocent, harmless mistake. Manny—who is not a native English speaker, but whose English is generally much better than he gives himself credit for—has sought the cliché, *you make your own destiny*, and instead has found something only slightly, but significantly, different. In a curious and wonderful way, he has looked to express an idea, a genuine feeling from a genuine moment in his life, but not finding the words directly, has (as all of us do at times) turned to the prepackaged axiom that comes closest to this feeling.

But he bobbles it a bit. He says (as all of us do at times) the wrong word. *Destination* instead of *destiny*. And in the process, he does exactly the opposite of what the cliché is intended to do, which is generalize into commonplace, and instead hits upon something perhaps much closer to the genuine idea and feelings he looked to express in the first place. (So very Manny of him.) His noble attempt at articulation has led him, in the exuberance of the moment, to an error, which has, in the earnestness that is Manny himself, led him to something much closer to the truth.

## Please, Stay Awhile

Of course, this truth is not entirely obvious at the moment. When we first hear his statement we do not immediately recognize it for the obvious reason that the rearranged phrase, *you make your own destination*, is not entirely true. The interpretation we take from the original phrase, *you make your own destiny*, implies a deterministic will enforced upon life. The idea suggests that we, and we alone, control the situations and circumstances of our own lives. (And one of the great by-products of Manny's reordering of this phrase is that it makes sense of a previously senseless cliché. *You make your own destiny* is one of those phrases that works much better on a poster than it does under a critical light. The very idea of destiny is that it is ready-made [or, predetermined], and set out for you before you even set out toward it. Therefore, it is impossible to make, to mold and create, as the phrase suggests. To make it would be to unmake it, destiny being something that you accept. A *destination*, on the other hand, as Manny suggests, is something that can be made.)

So *making your own destiny* rings as false to us as it does to Manny. Being a professional athlete (and one without a no-trade clause), Manny should understand that sometimes other people try very hard, and nearly succeed, in making your destination for you. Sometimes people try to make your destination somewhere, anywhere, other than Boston. Sometimes those same people try to make your destination Texas. Sometimes they succeed, and sometimes they come very close and fail, but in neither case does it seem that one has had much to do in the making of one's destination.

Manny, being Manny, should know all this after being placed on waivers in the '03/'04 baseball off-season. This move could have allowed any team in baseball to make his destination anywhere from Anaheim to Baltimore. Subsequently (when no one did), Manny was somewhat aggressively offered up in a trade between the Red Sox and Rangers that would have made his destination Arlington, Texas.

A good number of very smart people with a good deal of money spent a good deal of time and energy and ingenuity into making this destination for him; and yet, in the end, it did not work. (It was not, perhaps, destined to be.)

At the time, Manny, when asked about these efforts, expressed an acute ambivalence toward his own destination, saying, wisely, that if he stayed in Boston, he would play in Boston, and if he was sent to Texas, he would play in Texas. He accepted the fact that others had a hand in where he played baseball. It would thus seem that his statement on the clubhouse stage was in fact false. It could then be read as the convenient statement of a man for whom the independent forces of the Players' Association and experimental ankle surgery and solid postseason pitching have conspired (with his help) to bring him, conveniently, to the destiny he envisioned and now believes to have created all by himself.

But this assumption gives Manny both too much credit and far too little. The answer to whether he has, in fact, made his own destination is not found on that stage, but in understanding Manny's idea of a destination and what he has done to try and make it in the only arena he can—in the game, on the field, and in the batter's box.

## Come Watch Manny Swing

It is there, in the batter's box at Fenway, that we find him now, trying to make a destination for himself and for the Sox in Game One of the World Series. With one out in the top of the seventh and the Sox and Cardinals tied at seven, Manny takes a slow walk behind home plate and circles around to the batter's box, Fenway rallying around him.

It has been a cool and curious night at the ballpark to this point. The World Series festivities have spilled over into four Red Sox runs in the first, then three more in the third, only to have both cancelled out by a pair of Cardinals runs in the second and third, three in the fourth, and two more in the six, leveling the score at 7-7. With the game now sloping down its back third and its outs and opportunities diminishing with it, there is a rumble of urgency in the pleading cheers triggered by Manny's name over the public address.

Mark Bellhorn stands on second, Orlando Cabrera on first, and Manny at the plate, where he steps in with a tap of his black bat on the outside corner of home plate. He wears his long, baggy white pants down to the tops, and covering the heels, of his black spikes. Beneath his white jersey (the top button undone), he wears a red mock turtleneck, with two cream-colored sleeves on both elbows and two wide black wristbands (no. 24 on each) above his black batting gloves. He presses his helmet to his head with his right hand, shoots of shaggy black hair sprouting from either side, with a small patch of black on his chin and a thin stubble over his top lip. His mouth is calm; his eyes are large and lazy, comfortable and slightly detached from the electricity of both the stage and the situation.

Facing out to the mound and Cardinals reliever Kiko Calero, he swings his bat in one smooth counterclockwise arc and brings it silently to rest just above and just behind his back shoulder. Calero sets and delivers a fastball low and outside, and Manny makes only a slight, cursory flinch in its direction. Ball one. He steps back, presses the helmet in place, taps the bat to the corner of the plate, and steps back in (left, right) with one smooth arc of the bat to the back shoulder. He looks out, shoulders and hips square to the plate, front foot extended and toes pointed at the front of the stance, knees imperceptibly bent, eyes tired and quiet and relaxed as they look to the mound.

Calero sets, and as he kicks and delivers, Manny's front foot bobs an inch off the dirt and falls, releasing the stance. His hands drop and his head turns and his back leg pivots, the bat gliding into the zone as the front foot lands and ball, head, eyes, hands, and bat all meet over the inside half of the plate. The bat sails through, the hips sliding open as the front knee bends and the body leans forward and the bat completes its smooth clockwise arc, describing the ball as it shoots into the wide outfield gap in left center.

Bellhorn comes around to score, Cabrera plays a bad relay throw into an extra base and takes third, and Manny, caught now between first and second, turns and dives back into first (one of his destinations). We, at Fenway, rise and cheer one of the greatest hitters in the game and one of the most beautiful swings we have ever seen.

## *MONSTER* minutiae

Manny's swing is a breathtaking one, elegant as it is effective, and neither time nor repetition have dulled the pleasure we as Sox fans, as baseball fans, take in witnessing it. With zero wasted movements (as opposed to the swing of, say: Sheffield, Gary), the swing is a model of efficiency—the bat and body lift and lean back in one motion (inhale); the toe rises and falls; and the hands, head, shoulders, hips, and legs all glide in one fluid motion through the ball (exhale). Often called a quiet swing, the impression of tranquility reflects the way the bat does not so much seem to hit the ball as pass through it. Perfectly balanced, serenely graceful, and powerfully efficient, the swing suggests to us that this motion—this fluid set of movements—is exactly what the human body was designed to do all along.

It was not, of course, but then we would never know this from watching Manny swing, just as we never know from watching him that this elegant, graceful swing was not solely the product of superior talent, but, mostly, of hard work. Known by teammates for years, this work was one of the well-kept secrets throughout Manny's early years with the Red Sox (after he signed as a free agent in December of 2000). The details of his tremendous commitment to the swing and its improvement have been acknowledged publicly only recently.

We know now that he is one of the first to arrive at the ballpark, every day. We know that he spends hours in the batting cages beneath the Fenway bleachers, every day. And we know that this commitment to the swing and its improvement extends into and through the offseason. We know that the swing derives its elegance and grace not from within, but from repetition. Although it is still the highly attuned natural eye-mind-hand reactions that make the swing a tool for great things, the swing itself has been constructed by Manny, through a lifetime of hard work and commitment. He made it himself. The swing is one of Manny's destinations, one of the destinations he did in fact make, just as he made the 8-7 lead the Sox now enjoy in Game One thanks to his RBI single in the seventh.

## Come See Manny Field

But there are other destinations made by Manny, just as there are other innings in a game. The bottom of the seventh moves to the top of the eighth and Manny moves from the batter's box to left field, where his destination is somewhat less gracefully reached (but is breathtaking nonetheless). The Sox added another run in the seventh on an infield single by Ortiz and now lead 9-7 with six outs to go. Manny exchanges bat for glove and jogs out to left field, taking his position on the green grass with the high left field wall at his back.

Marlon Anderson grounds out to begin the inning, but is followed by a Mike Matheny single to center (bringing in pitcher Jason Marquis to pinch run) and a Roger Cedeno single to right, putting runners on second and third with one out and bringing Sox closer Keith Foulke into the game. Manny punches his glove and wanders around in left. Edgar Renteria steps in against Foulke and lines a single through the left side of the infield. Marquis breaks for third as the ball skips into the outfield and Manny charges in, sweeps his glove down over the grass to scoop the ball—only to skim it on his way by. He stops, lunges back, picks, and throws home as Marquis runs down the line, slides in, and is called safe. Varitek, Francona, and all of Fenway Park immediately disputed the call, and on replay, it appears as if Marquis did slide into Varitek's shinguard rather than the plate, which he swept over only *after* the tag. It is hard to tell, either way.

The play is ruled a single and an error (E7), and Manny wanders back into left, tugging at the end of his glove. The situation resets now, with Cedeno on second and Renteria on first and Larry Walker at the plate, still with only one out but now with the Cardinals trailing by only a run, at 9-8. Walker runs the count to 2-2, then clips a shallow, dying flare to left. Manny charges with hard, long, loping strides and arms out at his side. At the last instant, he pushes his right leg out to lead a quick slide under the ball, which now falls toward him and arrives the instant his right front cleats catch in the Fenway turf and buckle his left knee, vaulting body over leg as the ball bounces innocently at his side. Cedeno scores easily from second, tying the game. Manny, pulling himself up in left, brushes off his knee and pulls a clump of dirt and grass from his cleats. The play is scored an error (E7).

# *MONSTER* minutiae

Unlike the swing, Manny afield looks anything but fluid. All the grace and ease we find in him at the plate somehow slips away into the left field grass. Although he is not a bad fielder—he makes almost all the plays he should make, and occasionally a few that he has no business even trying to make—the head-shaking absurdity of the plays he does not make, and the inelegance with which he makes even routine plays, reinforce this image of a man out of sorts. Off balance, staggering, and often landing awkwardly, Manny's fielding seems to suggest to us that this action—running around an outfield trying to catch a baseball with a glove—was never what the human body was designed to do, ever.

Was it destiny—unlucky bounces of pure fate—that caused the two errors and the two runs? A case can be made, in both instances, that it was. The first ball skipped through the infield with a slight bounce and once it reached the outfield flattened, hugged the lush outfield grass, and darted under Manny's glove. The second seemed even more of a fluke, a characteristic slide that Manny has made routinely without such mishaps, only this time, he caught the exact right cleat at the exact right angle that anchored his foot rather than allowing it to glide across the grass.

But these arguments (like many made in defense of fate) wither and slip away in the October air as quickly as they are posed. Instead, we turn to the evidence and the man before us, and realize that, like the swing, the fielding is a product he has made. And more than the repetition of hitting, fielding in baseball is a product of instincts and decision-making. Somehow, the same instincts that allow Manny to instinctively recognize the location, speed, rotation, and movement of a 93-mph slider as it snaps through the strike zone keep him from recognizing that the ball off Walker's bat has enough loft to it for him to run under it, without sliding. The same decision-making that allows him to decide instantly to swing at the inside fastball fail him when he decides to slide under the shallow fly.

Manny recognized this much himself later on, and would admit as much after the game, when he told reporters that it was not the catching of the cleat that was the problem, but the decision to slide that led to the cleat catching. Had he not slid, he said, he would have caught the ball on the run, easy. The same went for the ball he overran, which he instinctively misjudged and then made the poor decision of trying to come up throwing before he had the ball, and therefore never got his glove to the ground. These mistakes were the products of Manny's actions in the field; the destinations he made for himself (and the tie game the destination he made for his teammates) as much as he made the RBI single a half inning earlier (which gave his team the lead).

## RED SOX NATION

Manny is the latest in a long line of great-hitting left fielders who have had to learn the peculiarities of the Wall in left—among them Ted Williams (1946–1960), Carl Yastrzemski (1961–1983), Jim Rice (1974–1989), and Mike Greenwell (1985–1996). Each spent several seasons adjusting to left field in Fenway, and it was anticipated from the very beginning that Manny would be no different. This has only proved partially true, though, because while Manny did struggle to adjust at first, he has since shown that when it comes to playing the field (whether struggling or not), no one has ever done it quite like Manny.

# Keep Moving, There's Plenty to See

How then, does Manny Ramirez move beyond these triumphs and failures to make another destination three nights later, in Game Three in St. Louis? (Where in the first inning he releases the swing on a 2-2 fastball from Jeff Suppan and launches the ball high and deep—a breathtaking drive—into the left field bleachers, giving the Sox a crucial early lead that they will never give up.) And how does he reach his and his team's ultimate destination the following night when they win the World Series and he wins its MVP?

Simple, really. By doing what he does, which is continue to play. Manny, it seems, is always at play somehow, whether on the field or off, during the game or otherwise; and yet this continuing on, continuing to do, is how he makes it to where he is going. A destination, after all, by its very definition, is the place to which a person travels. Therefore, the only way one can fail to make a destination is to stay in one place, physically or mentally.

How clearly, then, we see Manny, as he moves back and forth between the field and the plate, inning to inning, game to game, continuing to play. This is how he makes his destination, by not allowing himself to get caught up in what has happened, whether it be a failed attempt at trading him, a towering home run in a big game, or a foolish gaffe in a key situation. He lets it go, moves on, and by doing so makes himself a new destination every inning and every game. It is not always the destination he would prefer, but then sometimes it is. Either way, it is something he has made, something he has traveled to—a destination rather than a destiny.

# Now Sit Back, Relax, and Enjoy the Show

This word *destiny*, of course, had been a troubling one among Red Sox fans long before it troubled Manny in the World Series postgame. The idea that certain outcomes, certain scenarios, and certain ways in which the baseball world functions are somehow fixed and permanent, and exist independent of the generations of Red Sox players and staff who have worked to change them, has been a dangerous (and at times self-fulfilling) notion among the Red Sox and their fans.

Understandably so. Eighty-six years of reaching the same destination despite your best efforts is rather conveniently explained by a shrug and a tip of the cap to destiny—which so obviously had created this destination for the Red Sox and directed them to it year after year. *What can we do? We're the Sox, and Sox fans; it is simply our lot to suffer.* But this is not movement. This is stagnation. This is staying in one place—the only way possible to keep from changing one's destination.

Change is only possible when this idea of destiny is pushed aside, is denied, and the realization is made that one may be continuing to reach the same miserable destination because one is simply traveling down the wrong road. A new route is selected, and the first step toward a new destination is taken. This is how change is made, and this is what the Red Sox organization eventually did, what their fans eventually mimicked, and what Manny Ramirez has been doing all along.

You see, Manny—up there now on the stage in the St. Louis clubhouse, holding the shiny silver MVP trophy—has never stopped moving, not since he arrived in Boston. He has not always moved forward—at times, he has wandered a curious route (leaving us scratching our heads) and at times, he has moved backward (leaving us shaking our heads)—but through it all he has kept moving and never looked back. He has reached different destinations at different times, but the fact that he now stands in the center of a champagne-soaked celebration, holding the single greatest honor his profession can bestow upon an individual, is largely a product of his ability to leave his past destinations (be they triumphs or follies) behind him and to continue to move, to play. By doing so, he continues to make new destinations—fate and destiny be damned.

And so as we watch him there, quietly smiling as we correct the slip in his second-language cliché, we realize (as he gives another point and smile salute across the clubhouse) that it is not he, but we, who need correcting. Destiny has never been the right word for moments such as these; moments that have taken so much work and striving to achieve, and over which such a very long road has been traveled to reach.

And so no, Manny, we will not correct you here, will not whisper that *destiny* is the word we think you meant. Instead, we smile with you and nod, and say, yes, Manny, you were right all along—you do, after all, make your own destination.

**idiot RULE:** *From Manny himself:*
*You make your own destination.*

# Chapter 3

# Big Papi Rises Up

**Cold and lifeless,** the quiet grandstands of Fenway empty under a light drizzle as the final half-inning of Game Three of the ALCS opens, leaving the last solitary figures scattered among wide swaths of empty red seats, elbows on knees, chins in hand, staring blankly in the direction of third base.

When the first out is recorded, a pair of friends drop their empty wrappers and cups under their seats, stuff their hands in jacket pockets, and shuffle down the steps. A few moments later, after the third and final out of the night, these solitary figures remain, chins in hand, and stare blankly across the field under a chilly drizzle, silent and motionless as the cluster of white digits on the scoreboard slip out of focus. Later, without word or gesture, they stand and leave, and behind them the ballpark is left silent and empty, and in time each of the high light banks disappear into the dark sky with a soft thud, and Fenway Park falls into darkness for the night.

## The Ballpark Under Nightfall

It is always an oddly inappropriate sight, the ballpark under nightfall—the scoreboards and signs turned off, the bullpens and dugouts cleared, the windows of the clubs and press box and the long rows of suites stretching out around them faceless and blank. The bleachers are an empty triangle, the field a gray-green void, the grandstands an arch of shadow with a dull glow from the streetlights on Yawkey falling through the gates above the third base side, reflecting off the standing puddles in the walkway. Above all, it is quiet—a siren on Park Drive, two blocks away, calls through the right field concourse and slips across the field. The ballpark that has drawn in so much energy is now a sudden, startling void among the rhythms and chorus of its city. Such a void is not so much left as drained, and on this night, of all nights, the old ballpark sits drained down to its steel beams and old brick walls, devoid of sound, movement, or light—and nearly, nearly lifeless.

But not yet. In a few hours, a group of men and women appear from the dark concourses onto moonlit ramps, and pull hoses and buckets and large plastic bins into the grandstands. With powerful jets of water, they begin to wash away the night, pushing free the piles of peanut wrappers, crumpled plastic cups, and tattered programs.

Trucks begin to line up on Ipswich Street, unloading racks of hot dog buns and steel kegs of beer. A few hours later, the first worn sneakers of the grounds crew step onto the dewy grass of the outfield, and familiar faces arrive in offices and sit down at desks. Phones begin to ring, coffee begins to brew, televisions are turned on, and newspapers are unfolded. Cooks and cameramen, journalists and publicists, pitchers and catchers, bartenders and ushers all arrive at the ballpark. Under the late afternoon sun, the first soft thwack of a wooden bat hitting a baseball echoes through the concourses as batting practice begins.

A few hours later, the gates open, and turnstiles click 34,826 clicks to let 34,826 fans into the ballpark, where they are handed fresh bags of peanuts, crisp new programs, and full plastic cups before being ushered to their red plastic seats. They sit as the players take the field, and the tall, lean man on the mound takes a small step back and delivers, and Fenway Park comes to life for one more game.

## Red Sox v. Yankees, Once More

Sixty-nine outs later, the fourth game of the American League Championship Series has yet to be decided. The scoreboard equation stands balanced across eleven and a half frames at 4/4 (2 + 2 across the top, 3 + a lone, distant 1 across the bottom). The same lone figures sit in the same red seats, elbows on knees, chins in hand, staring blankly in the direction of third base. There have been flickers of life throughout the night, but the drain of the previous week and shock of the previous night has left them with their hands clutched together, staring out at the field, unblinking. The public address announcer calls out, *now batting for the Red Sox, the designated hitter, number 34, David Ortiz.*

A nervous, measured applause rises throughout Fenway as the large man in the on-deck circle stabs the end of his bat to the ground, knocking off its ring of weight, and takes one heavy step after another toward the plate.

## RED SOX NATION

When David Ortiz first stepped to the plate for the Sox, his large frame and leaning, crouching stance brought to mind the image of a former left-handed Sox slugger—Mo Vaughn (1991–1998). Like Ortiz, Vaughn was the type of dangerous hitter who combined both power and discipline, and both quickly became the man Sox fans wanted to see at the plate with the game on the line. However, it has been off the field, in the clubhouse and the community, where the two are most analogous. Vaughn is still remembered for his leadership among teammates and generous contributions within the community; likewise, conversations about Ortiz tend to naturally find their way from the player on the field to the character of the man off the field.

He wears all white, all the way down to his black shoe tops, with a brace of black armor on his right elbow, black wristbands on both fore-arms, and red gloves on both hands as he drags his black bat behind him. Under the bill of his dark helmet, we see his broad, round face, the wide mouth and eyes too big for the helmet, too big for the face, too big for the ballpark. He grabs the bat and steps in, left foot first with a quick twist of the toe in the dirt, then a tap of the bat to the plate as the right foot follows and the bat is pulled back. Both knees bend as his shoulders tilt forward to the mound. He leans the bat in, waves it, and with helmet, face, and eyes steady, straight ahead, he waits. He takes a ball, then a strike, then a ball in the dirt. He steps out, stands up straight and leans the bat between his legs as he holds both hands up, palms out, and spits once, quickly, on his red batting glove. He rubs the two open palms together and grabs the handle of the bat. He steps back in, and with our elbows on our knees, and hands clutched before us, we fix our tired eyes on his stance, and on his waving bat.

We close our eyes (*please*) and open them the instant the pitch flies and Ortiz swings and in one deep arc, lifts the ball into the air and lifts every Red Sox fan on the planet into one long, wild, jumping, shouting celebration. Fenway erupts under the bright lights and somewhere above it all, music plays—first a familiar bass line, then a voice calls out and says he wants to tell us a story, says it's all about our town—and we know this story and we know this town and sing along in agreement that *yeah, we love that dirty water.* And as the big man in white rounds the bases and we stand and sing with eyes wide open (*thank you*), the mad rollicking scene around home plate blurs as we stare into it to find the one man who has suddenly changed everything.

## The Compassion of David Ortiz

Later, with the shouts from the lingering celebration still echoing through the grandstands, a reporter asked Ortiz a question about how he felt coming to the ballpark that afternoon, knowing the season could end that very night. Arms folded on the white pressroom table and leaning over the tiny microphone in front of him, Ortiz replied with a story. In his deep, measured English, he said that he had seen the faces at Fenway the night before, after Game Three. He had seen tears in a fan's eyes, and on the way to the ballpark that day, he had thought about those tears, and about how he did not want those people to be crying anymore. That was all. And we, his listening audience, sat in quiet awe.

So often, these predictable questions are asked just to receive the predictable answer. In this situation—with a team defeated, humiliated, on the verge on catastrophe—the expected response is that of personal, professional dignity. The player and his team do not want to be embarrassed, and the reporter tries to appeal to his and their pride, wants Ortiz to say that they had to fight back. They had to show a little backbone, show a little dignity, show a little bit of pride.

How strange is it, then, when we learn that the giant, powerful hero of this grand moment, the man who has won the game and who has so very much to be proud of, was not motivated by swelling pride, but, instead, by compassion. Other athletes tell more general stories, and make broader claims—they want to win it for the fans, the best fans in the world, and so on.

Yet these claims too often sound hollow, rehearsed; too convenient among the interlaced boasts of pride and purpose. Ortiz's story had none of these trappings. He did not claim to comprehend the suffering of all Red Sox fans and likewise his story was no epic. It was, on the contrary, the expression of a very simple, very commonplace, very basic human act: one person empathizing with another—simple, selfless, and giving. The home run made Big Papi a hero, but this, the compassion of David Ortiz himself, is what made him heroic.

## CURSE BUSTERS

One detail we will, only now, privately smile upon, is the fact that in the end, Ortiz did not stop the tears of Red Sox fans at Fenway. Those same eyes that cried long and hard after Game Three cried just as long and just as hard after Game Four, too. What Big Papi did was change the expression behind them. That was all—but that was everything.

## Back at It

And so once again, the last fans trickle out of Fenway and onto the streets. Once again, the lights are turned out and the gates locked, and a few hours later a group of men and women appear from the dark concourses onto moonlit ramps, pull hoses and buckets and large plastic bins into the grandstands, and wash away the night.

Once again, the trucks begin to line up in the early dawn hours along Ipswich Street. Once again, the first worn sneakers of the grounds crew step on the dewy grass of the outfield. The familiar faces all arrive and shake hands and smile as phones begin to ring, coffee begins to brew, televisions are clicked on, and newspapers are snapped open. Cooks and cameramen, journalists and publicists, pitchers and catchers, bartenders and ushers all arrive and shrug (*back again, huh, one more time*) to each other. Under the late afternoon the first soft thwack of a wooden bat hitting a baseball, mixed in with laughter, echoes through the concourses as batting practice begins.

A few hours later the gates open, and the turnstiles click 35,120 clicks to let 35,120 fans into the ballpark, where they are handed fresh bags of peanuts, crisp new programs, and full plastic cups before being ushered to their red plastic seats, clean and dry. They shake hands with a neighbor as the players take the field, and the small, slender pitcher on the mound takes a step back and delivers. Fenway Park comes to life, once again, for one more game.

## Red Sox v. Yankees, Once More with Feeling

Eighty-three outs later, the fifth game of the American League Championship Series has yet to be decided. The scoreboard equation is balanced across thirteen and a half frames at 4/4 (1 + 3 across the top, 2 + 2 spread far apart across the bottom). The same crowd leans in, elbows to knees, weary and worn. The collective wear of the previous thirteen innings, the previous four games, the previous season, and the previous 86 years has exhausted the faces, stiffened the legs, and numbed the hearts and hands of those who now lean in and give quick, encouraging claps and strained, hoarse shouts to the man at the plate. *Come on now, Johnny, get us going.*

When he does, when Johnny Damon walks, and Manny follows with another walk, and suddenly, a moment later, the announcer calls once again, *Now batting for the Red Sox, the designated hitter, number 34, David Ortiz*, it takes genuine effort to lift up out of our seats, to stand and call out, *Come on, Papi.* The large man in the on-deck circle stabs the end of his bat to the ground, knocking off its ring of weight, and takes one heavy step after another toward the plate. He rests the bat between his legs, spits on his batting gloves, rubs both open palms together, and grabs the handle of the bat as he steps into the box, left foot followed by right. He sets his stance and looks out to the mound, to Yankees pitcher Esteban Loaiza. Loaiza gets his sign, nods, and delivers the first pitch of the at-bat.

## The At-Bat

Ortiz swings through it for strike one.

Ortiz watches the second pitch go by, a ball up and away, and we give a quick clap and we think about how a walk would be all right here, how we would have the bases loaded with two outs and Millar up.

Ortiz swings at the third pitch and fouls it off for strike two, and suddenly we desperately need him to get a hit here, to win the game and send us and the Sox back to New York, where we'll have Schilling going in Game Six. If Schill can be effective and we can somehow find a way to win that game, then it would be on to Game Seven, where anything could happen, anything at all.

Ortiz swings and fouls off the fourth pitch, and we gradually allow ourselves to think about what it would be like to come back and beat the Yankees in Game Seven, to win the ALCS after being down 3-0. How perfect would it be to force such a fate on the team by which we had suffered such a fate so many times before, for their humiliation to allow our triumph into the World Series? We think about this and we begin to see how easily it could all be done—we could win this game and win the ALCS and then go on, go farther, and win the World Series. The Red Sox could win the World Series, still. They could win it *this* year and this very month, and suddenly we rip four hard claps out and shout with everything we have left, *Come on, Big Papi.*

Ortiz swings and fouls the fifth pitch off the outside corner, away, and we begin to see a golden trophy, shining through a champagne shower. We begin to think of all the years we have done this, all the games we have sat here and watched, all the afternoons we have tuned in and paced our living rooms. We think about the people we have watched with, about the people we have comforted after a rough loss and, more dearly, the people who have comforted us after the roughest of losses. Looking back, we see a lifetime of following and discussing and debating, of cheering and shouting, of standing with arms up and slouching down with head in hands. We begin to trace our history with this game and this team, and connect it to the trophy still shining through that champagne shower. And somehow it all seems to fit; it all seems to make sense when lined up just so. The only piece that has been missing all this time was this at-bat, right here, with the Sox and Yankees tied at Fenway and a runner on second and the right man standing at the plate. Ortiz watches the sixth pitch go by, outside, for ball two. He steps back, spits on his gloves, smacks them and twists both open palms together, grabs the bat, and steps back into the box. As he does, we glance out at Damon on second, and then back to Papi at the plate, and suddenly in the cold October air, all we want is for this season not to end, for this team that we have followed since February to continue on together. This is what is most important to us, right now, only that baseball should continue on, and that this season should not end here.

Ortiz swings at the seventh pitch, outside, and fouls it off, steadying the count at 2-2. As we look out across the field to the gray-clad Yankees fielders, we refine our wish even further. We now leave history and the World Series trophy behind, and focus on our deep, abiding desire to beat the Yankees. We clutch our hands and think of all the times we have watched them celebrate while we sunk our heads in silence; of all the signs and all the dusty video clips and all the laughing, knowing smirks; and as we exhale and shake our heads, we dismiss the years of waiting. We instead turn only to what is most important to us, right here, at this moment—this series, and this one opponent, and this rivalry, and how desperately we want this long, ridiculous history of nonsense to finally and abruptly end.

## *MONSTER* minutiae

Fans learn quickly not to pray for miracles. The 5'10" utility infielder pinch-hitting in the ninth is not, in all likelihood, going to crush a towering three-run HR off the opposing ace, so we better not pray for it, and instead look for a single or even a walk. We only ask what the player is capable of. Big Papi, however, has become that rare player who is not only capable of miracles, but relatively efficient at producing them. Over his first two seasons in Boston, he has provided the big hit in the big situation enough times to convince his fans of this, and by doing so has allowed Sox fans free range to pray for whatever it is they need at the moment. Home run? Grand slam? No line for the restroom? With Ortiz at the plate, anything is possible. (*Come on, Big Papi.*)

Ortiz swings and fouls off the eighth pitch, a ball off the outside corner, and a few fans in the sections below us rise to their feet and shout encouragement to the man at the plate. We realize with a quick glance around the ballpark what a game this has been, what a collection of plays and players, of moments and memories, and how this one game, because of its significance and its drama, may be the greatest baseball game we have ever witnessed, perhaps the greatest game we will ever witness. No equal comes to mind, not here in Fenway, where we have sat so often and watched for so long, where so many games have ended with a sigh and a shrug and a long walk through the dark concourse. Then, suddenly, we forget about Games Six and Seven, and leave them and the series and the Yankees for another day, and instead turn everything in on this one game, this one night at Fenway. This game, then, is all that matters in all of the hundreds of games we have watched and attended, only this one matters, here, tonight; the Sox simply have to win this game—it is all we ask for.

Ortiz swings at the ninth pitch, a ball low and away, and fouls it off, and suddenly we realize, as more fans rise to their feet, that this has been one hell of an at-bat. After getting ahead in the count, Loaiza has fought to stay away from Ortiz. He's pounded the outside corner of the plate with fastballs trying to get Ortiz to chase, and either miss it or pop it up over the infield. Loaiza has relentlessly tried to run one by him, but Ortiz has fought hard, fouled off pitch after pitch, protecting the plate and trying to force Loaiza back over the plate; one pitch after another, back and forth. The pitcher is determined and the batter disciplined and unyielding and *good God* this is why we love baseball, this is why we have watched all these years—this series of battles between pitcher and batter—this is what the game begins with and what it comes down to, and everything else fills in around it as the man with the ball tries to figure out how to throw it by a man with a bat.

And at this moment all we really want, as we stand with the rest of Fenway, is for the man with the bat to win this battle, for him to stay disciplined, for him to continue to fight, for him to dig in and look out to the mound and resolve to foul off 100 fastballs away 100 times before he gives in and tries to pull one. All we want right at this moment, and nothing else—not history, the season, the series, or even the game—matters as much as for David Ortiz to get this one hit, this one time, in this one at-bat. With everything we have, we give two quick claps and shout, *Come on, Big Papi, one time*, and clutch our hands together, close our eyes for one beat, and open them just as Loaiza delivers.

Ortiz swings at the tenth pitch, his pitch, inside and over the plate, and pulls his hands back through the zone and muscles the ball out into the field and up over the mound, drifting, with just enough sail to clear the infield and land with a soft bounce in the shallow outfield grass; and all at once the tired and weary at Fenway and in Boston and throughout New England all burst into one vibrant surge of life— shouting and laughing and hugging and, for some down in the aisle and out in the streets of Boston, dancing.

## The Ballpark Revived

It is this moment that is why David Ortiz is Big Papi, it is this moment that he has given to Red Sox fans everywhere and for which he will always be remembered. He will be remembered, surely, as part of the team that won Games Four and Five of the ALCS at Fenway and went on to win Games Six and Seven at Yankee Stadium. He will be remembered as part of the team that won all four games of the World Series, and held above them a shining gold trophy.

His broad smile and lazy, lumbering walk are as much a part of these memories as any other, but his place among this group of players and games will always stand out for the celebrations he began and the joy he gave to all those who celebrated along with him. Because while baseball in general, and Red Sox baseball in particular, is a game that lives on in our memories as a collection of events and images, it is still, at its core, a game of moments. The history of the game is made up of a series of seasons, each season made up of a series of games, each game made up of a series of innings, each inning made up of a collection of at-bats, and each at-bat a collection of pitches; each pitch and each swing a moment. At their very best, these moments are capable of sparking delight and joy and a wild, rejoicing celebration in which nothing else matters and of which few moments in life are capable of duplicating. It is this moment, then, this moment of pure delight in life, that David Ortiz has given Fenway Park and Red Sox fans everywhere.

As we glance out to him now, rounding first and watching Damon sprint home, his teammates burst from the dugout to mob him on the infield. We imagine him offering up this moment to his teammates and us with the same compassion he offered the night before, not wanting to see any more tears in the stands. Instead, he tells all of us to stand and cheer one more time; to high-five a stranger; to call someone we care about and shout into the phone; to laugh and dance and hear the music sounding out throughout the brilliantly lit, raucously rolling, and vibrantly alive Fenway Park; to listen to that story one more time, all about our town, and to go on ahead now, and sing about that dirty water.

**idiot RULE:** *Rise up, one game at a time.*

# Chapter 4

# Night at the Varitek Symphony Orchestra (VSO)

**Our seats for Game Two** of the World Series are in the bleachers, in straightaway center, and as the Red Sox complete their infield warmups and the umpire and pitcher take their positions, and we wait a moment for an invisible commercial to end, the view we are offered of Fenway is that of the few anxious moments before the curtain rises on a somewhat large-scale symphonic production. Our perspective on this scene is from backstage, of course, as we face the gallery and balcony levels shifting in their seats, a few late arrivals being just now quickly ushered down to their seats, programs in hand.

We see that this old auditorium is still very much open-air (on this cold, misty evening of huddled sweatshirts and gloves) and that it has been ceremoniously decked with red, white, and blue bunting at both the box seats and the mezzanine level; that its stage is well lit; and that the performance itself has been highly anticipated (a revival, if you will), for it is very much a full house. The musicians have taken their places in the orchestra, facing away from us and toward the audience in the grandstand as they shift and shuffle, adjust and readjust their instruments, in position and yet in constant motion. We glance across them, hardly needing our program at this point in the season, and start close to the stage, to our right, with Bill Mueller (among the clarinets) backing up on the dirt behind third base; next to him, we see Orlando Cabrera (our first violin for the evening) who wanders toward second then hops back two paces; across from him, Mark Bellhorn (on oboe) paces with his head down, brushing dirt from side to side; and completing the first row is Kevin Millar (on first trumpet), spitting into the infield grass and punching his glove around first.

Ranging behind, in the back row, we find our rhythm section wandering across the stage. To our immediate left we see Trot Nixon (on snare drums) worrying his small circle of stage; while almost directly beneath us, Johnny Damon (on bass drums) steps in a few paces, then backs up; and to our immediate right we find a crowd favorite, Manny Ramirez (our sometimes off-rhythm but always smashing cymbalist) picking at a string of leather on the back of his glove. (Somewhere offstage, we are told Mr. Ortiz, on stand-up double bass, is waiting for his cameo appearance.)

This is our orchestra for the evening, prepared to ably back the evening's star performer, Curt Schilling (the celebrated guest vocalist), who now stands with his back to us on a small, slightly elevated platform, front and center. The only figure remaining in this scene is also the only one who faces us, and the only figure who stands completely still among this anxious, shifting ensemble. He is the tall, solid figure at the front of the stage with his back to the audience, thick mitt in one hand and steel mask in the other; he is our catcher and conductor for the evening. *Ladies and gentlemen, won't you please welcome* Mr. Jason Varitek.

## Introducing the Catcher

It certainly would not be the same show without him. For the past six years, Jason Varitek—the strong, silent leader of this generation of Red Sox baseball—has stood front and center on this stage and given direction. As his place on the stage suggests, this 2004 team has quite literally been built around him. On this field, only Trot Nixon's pair of games at the very end of the 1996 season precede Varitek's arrival in Boston; but since the July '97 trade that brought both him and batterymate Derek Lowe from Seattle, Jason Varitek has been the man giving on-field direction to the Boston Red Sox.

It is a role he has grown into. When he arrived in his first full spring training in the majors, a twenty-six-year-old rookie with exactly one major league at-bat (and hit) to his credit, Varitek inherited more or less the same team that had gone 78-84 and finished in 4th place in 1997—a mismatched team with a cluster of aging veterans, a few rising stars, and far too many semi-anonymous journeymen. He may have been encouraged, however, by at least one familiar face—former Georgia Tech teammate and freshly minted AL Rookie of the Year, Nomar Garciaparra—and, perhaps more so, by one new acquaintance, new arrival and future batterymate Pedro Martinez. (We would like to think, looking back, that both men understood the significance of their introduction and first handshake.)

That season, as Varitek split time with incumbent Scott Hatteberg, the Sox began to turn things around, going 92-70 to finish 2nd in the AL East and earn a Wild Card berth, thus beginning the process that would eventually lead to St. Louis, and end on October 27, 2004. First though, Alan Embree was traded for in 2002 and Mike Timlin (never far behind) was signed later that year, and both met Varitek on the mound. Curt Schilling knew who his catcher would be when he signed on in late November of 2003, and so did Keith Foulke when he signed two weeks later. Everyone understood then. Everyone was aware. Every member of the 2004 World Champion Sox arrived in Boston with the same understanding of who No. 33 was, of who would be standing behind the plate, and who would be calling the signals.

## Leading with the Mind

Like all great conductors, Varitek's work has been late to receive recognition, for several reasons but primarily because the majority of what he provides for the team goes largely unseen and unheard by the audience. As he pulls on his mask and crouches down, red chest protector bracketed by red shin guards, the audience turns its attention to the small, elevated platform at center stage, where Schilling, the soloist, begins his performance (the second movement of his now famous opera).

But from our vantage point behind the stage, we continue to watch Varitek, to watch the direction he gives, and as Cardinals shortstop and leadoff man Edgar Renteria steps to the plate, we watch Varitek flash a set of signs, then punch his glove and settle into a crouch. The pitch is a fastball, low and away for strike one; Varitek steps, throws, and settles back into his crouch. The at-bat and inning continue on, and we are reminded of an aspect within this game that we often overlook: No. 33 is the only man on the field who is required to make creative decisions, who thinks of the game in terms of flow, and pace, and movement. He is the only one who is not reacting, but acting. The man on the mound, of course, lays some claim to this process, but he still takes his directional cues (like a musician from a good conductor) from his catcher. It is Varitek, however, who occupies the more cerebral position, creating the game from a blank page, pitch by pitch.

Over the seasons and during this first belabored inning (Renteria is eventually retired after twelve pitches), Varitek has orchestrated these finely balanced at-bats, innings, and games with a depth of intelligence and a complexity of craft that most fans (and many players) can only begin to understand. With a library of books and binders and notebooks piled away in his locker, and with both opponent and soloist in mind (for both are equally important to his work), he has produced the gameplans and strategies that have guided Red Sox pitching to the form it ultimately reached, here in the World Series, reaching its peak level of performance at the exact peak of the season—just, we assume, as Varitek planned it.

## RED SOX NATION

All Red Sox catchers are, at some point, measured against Carlton Fisk (1971–1980), and perhaps none have ever stood quite as tall against the Sox legend as Jason Varitek. Throughout his career, his toughness and ability both behind the plate and at bat have made these comparisons a justifiable topic. But when he said *enough* to the Yankees and brought his glove into A-Rod's face, he perhaps drew himself alongside Fisk—the catalyst of another memorable Sox-Yankees brawl—even closer.

Occasionally, throughout an inning and throughout the season, we notice with a flash of comprehension some small glimpse of this craft. We see the sequence of three pitches aligned to set up the fourth. We see how the sequence of three at-bats, all of which are loaded with fastballs, all work to set up the fourth, where the off-speed pitch in the dirt produces the crucial, game-ending strikeout. We see the small hop inside, the glove punch that alerts the hitter to Varitek's presence on the inside corner, and tips him off to the hard fastball on the hands that will surely follow, then watch as just before the delivery, Tek slides silently to the outside edge of the plate, framing the breaking ball away at which the hitter helplessly flails and instantly shoots a glance back to the catcher (*Hey, wait, I thought that—*). We are pleased with ourselves for noticing these small, subtle movements. But they are only movements; they are not the symphony.

Of the larger work, we can only piece together a few rather obvious rhythms—the early establishment of a certain pitch, the addition of a third pitch once the lineup turns over for its second at-bats—and nothing more. But perhaps it is better this way. Perhaps the mystery of how these small movements and steady rhythms work together to form something larger and more infinitely complex (the masterfully pitched game) is better left in the mind and crowded binders of its composer. Genius, after all, does not need to be understood to be appreciated; it only needs to be recognized. And so as Bill Mueller snags the final out of the first, and Varitek sprints off the field, helmet backwards and mask in hand, it seems enough to recognize that the apparently random sequence of pitches that have produced this scoreless inning have not, in fact, been so random after all. Instead, their order and rhythm and timing have all been meticulously composed, and deftly directed, by the watchful presence of our conductor behind the plate.

Then, he grabs a bat.

## Leading with a Very Large Wooden Bat

Because although catchers and leaders are required to exercise a studied and subtle mental clarity in certain areas of their work, they are, in certain other areas, required to exercise tremendous physical dexterity and force. Smashing baseballs into the deepest regions of Fenway Park is specifically one of these areas, and with that in mind, Varitek must put aside his composed gameplan for a moment, put on a helmet, and step up to the plate.

He does just this with two outs in the bottom of the first, with Manny standing on second and Ortiz standing on first, and with Cardinals' starter Matt Morris standing on the mound, looking more than a bit hassled. Varitek marches to the plate—quick strides on thick, powerful legs, his shoulders broad, his elbows slightly away from his body—and we see him for the first time without his catcher's gear: red socks pulled knee-high, red sleeves to his white batting gloves and covered on his right elbow by a black brace, the red of his turtleneck covering his thick neck to his full face and thick chin-covering goatee.

With both hands on his bat he knocks the dirt off the inside of his cleats, then steps in and sets his stance, feet slightly more than shoulder-width apart, front foot slightly open to the first base side (a switch hitter, he hits left-handed against the righty Morris) and rocking up and down on his toes. He swings two slow, deliberate waves toward the mound and raises the bat high above and behind his back shoulder, waving it there. The bat head swirls in the air, the front shoulder wavers back and forth, the front toe taps up and down. The entire stance gives the impression of a rather large, rather twitchy predator being restrained by some unseen leash, who at any moment might break free and do unspeakable harm to whatever object (be it baseball or thirdbaseman) may be in its path.

No wonder Morris looks hassled. Besides Varitek at the plate, and Manny and Ortiz behind him, he has established a rather stressful habit early in the game; after recording the first two outs, he managed to get ahead of both Manny and Ortiz 0-2 before walking both. Now he finds himself in the same position with Varitek, whom he has gotten down 0-2 as well (a swing and a foul), before delivering his third pitch, a low ball. He steps back to the mound and at this moment (no doubt with Manny and Ortiz on his mind) decides to come after Varitek, to challenge him.

# MONSTER minutiae

As Tim McCarver pointed out, the 2004 Red Sox led the league (once again) in man-hugs. Another category they may have led was dance routines—elaborate pre-rehearsed hand/foot-slap-shake maneuvers. Varitek, however, would have none of it. Definitely no dancing, and no hugs unless it's his wife or his mother. Everyone else better just knock fists, because that's all Varitek will allow before he grabs his chest protector and prepares for the next inning.

Varitek takes his two slow waves to the mound, lifts the bat, and begins his fidgety rocking and twirling, and coils back as Morris delivers and the pitch flies and all the twitching stills to one swift movement (as the leash snaps), the swing smooth and powerful as it smashes a low breaking ball deep into center. The ball rockets into the centerfield triangle, ricocheting off the wall near the 420 ft. sign and Varitek rounds first and digs to second with long, loping strides, arms out to his side and locked at the elbows; Manny scores; Varitek picks up Dale Sveum and now sprints for third as the ball comes in to short and Ortiz scores and Varitek slides into third on his seat, shoulders up, arms raised high, he pops up on the bag with a triple, having given the Sox an invaluable 2-0 lead in the first inning of Game Two. Brains and brawn, mind and matter, glove and bat, the catcher and leader does it all, and does it all in the only place where it all matters—on the field.

## The Catcher Takes a Bow

Over the course of the season, much was made of Varitek and his leadership, and even more so over the course of the playoffs, and yet little was made of the actual nature of this leadership. He handles pitchers well. He is a strong presence in the clubhouse. His teammates respected him. All admirable qualities, and yet all qualities of someone who might as easily follow as lead. This imprecision is understandable, of course; leadership is not an easy concept to define, and besides that, there are many different ways one can lead, not all of which are completely visible to anyone but those being led. The more visible leaders use words, rallying those around them with spirit and commotion (see: Tejada, Miguel).

Others lead by example, by going about their business and conducting themselves in the way that is expected to be followed, by setting themselves up as a shining model to be emulated (see: Jeter, Derek). Varitek has at times led by his words, saying only what needs to be said only when it needs to be said, and he has at times led by example, but in addition to these, he has led in quite a different way. At times, most of the time, perhaps, he has led by the sheer presence of his will. Unlike others (and unlike the above two shortstops), Varitek has led simply by standing tall behind the plate, and in the dugout, and in the clubhouse. His words are respected, his actions valued, but it is his drive that fuels the leadership quality so many have so accurately observed.

We can sense it ourselves, all the way out here in the centerfield bleachers, the determination of a man who will simply never quit working, who will simply never quit battling, who will simply never, ever back down from a challenge. It is captivating, even out here in the bleachers, to realize how a man standing still behind the plate and facing his team commands the attention and respect not only of his teammates, not only of the umpire behind him and the batter at his side, but of the entire audience as well. The ballpark waits for him, is led by him, and nothing begins until he decides, until he pulls on his mask, crouches down, and punches his glove.

## MONSTER minutiae

We have always known that Varitek would be the last to ever stand down in the face of a challenge, but until July 24, 2004, we had never actually seen it enacted. On that day, Alex Rodriguez made a series of very bad choices. He learned what the rest of us have always known: that while there may be members of the Red Sox you could get away with shouting at, a few who might laugh at you or shrug it off, when it comes to Varitek, you should not expect such courtesies. If one should continue to shout a certain word at a Sox pitcher, and if one should be so foolish as to shout this same word at Varitek himself, repeatedly, you should expect a thick leather catcher's mitt and a thick fist shoved into your face—hard. By doing all of this, Alex Rodriguez learned a lesson we do not anticipate any American League hitter requiring a refresher on any time soon, and that is the fact that Jason Varitek will not back down.

In the end, when the show was finally over three nights later in St. Louis, two distinct images of Varitek made the front pages of the Boston papers the following morning. The cover of the *Boston Globe* showed the moment after the final out, the beginning of the celebration, as a leaping Jason Varitek and a high-flying Doug Mientkiewicz both flew into Foulke's arms to form the center of the Red Sox mob that would amass around them an instant later. The full-page cover of the *Boston Herald* showed the opposite end of the celebration, in the clubhouse later on, where a champagne-drenched Varitek—already by that time in championship T-shirt and hat—balanced the shining gold World Champions trophy on top of his head.

But in between these two loud, laughing and smiling images there was another moment that did not make the cover of either paper, but which was both less expected and more meaningful. The moment came shortly after the initial mob on the field had broken up, as teammates and coaches embraced and pulled T-shirts on and embraced family. As they did, Jason Varitek, the catcher and leader, broke off from the pack and staggered to an empty patch of grass just in front of home plate, where he collapsed to his knees and bowed his head to the ground—overwhelmed by the moment. No one knows (no one *could* know) what thoughts passed through his mind at the moment. The grinding exertion of hard work and determination and sheer will that the man had exerted in an effort to reach this very point are of a magnitude and weight that few of us can even begin to fathom.

All we can ever know of this moment, as we see No. 33 knelt down there on the grass, head to the ground, is that this weight, no matter how heavy or difficult it became to bear throughout the years, was never too much for him. He withstood it all. He provided the direction and presence this talented team so desperately needed every game and every inning until the final out, when the man who stood so tall for Boston for so long finally knelt to the ground and bowed his head to the grass, having done all we ever asked him to do.

**idiot RULE:** *Please do not taunt the catcher.*

# Chapter 5

# Nixon in Purgatory

**With two outs** in the bottom of the third, with the Red Sox up 3-0 in the World Series and up 1-0 in this, its fourth game, and with Bill Mueller tossing his bat aside and jogging down to first after ball four has loaded the bases, Trot Nixon is exactly where he is supposed to be. Bat dragging at his side, he walks with short, slightly pigeon-toed steps from the on-deck circle to the left batters' box at home plate. On the mound, Cardinals starter Jason Marquis receives the ball back from his catcher and shakes his head, not quite as nervous (or at least not appearing so) as he should be. Although the Cardinals are only down a run, he has lived a dangerous life over the first three innings, falling behind 16 out of the 19 hitters he has faced and running up a considerable debt in the accounting department of baseball fortune. Nixon, however, is still owed a bit in those books. (*Perhaps more than a bit.*)

## First Impressions

A thick, compact player who carries most of his weight (and most of his power) in his legs, Nixon cuts a disheveled figure against the crisp, ironed white-and-reds of the Cardinals. He wears a black shin guard on his right ankle, twisted to face the mound, and a red wristband on his left forearm. The left sleeve of his gray jersey is partially covering the tight, cream-colored sleeve he wears over his left elbow, and both black batting gloves are loaded with the pine tar he has caked on his nearly-black helmet. His scrappy handlebar mustache, which is surrounded by a day's growth of stubble, is not quite trim, and the expression on his face, even now, is of a slight boredom born from repetition. Every at-bat, the expression is the same—the only facial expression a hard blink, followed occasionally by thumb and forefinger reaching up to his cheeks, prying his eyes open a bit wider and blinking hard, as if his eyes were perpetually dusty. He cups his helmet in his left hand (it sticks like a suction cup) and removes it, holds the handle of his bat in his right and pulls his arm up, wipes his brow with the inside of his right sleeve, then repeats, wiping his brow with the inside of his left elbow before popping the helmet back on and securing it with one, firm press to the back. He grabs the bat with both hands, and as he steps into the box with his left foot, it is exactly where he is supposed to be at this moment—the situation he has imagined himself in all summer long, and at this moment there seems no possible alternative. This is Trot Nixon's at-bat. But as Red Sox fans know, and as Nixon himself is more aware of than anyone, his walk to the batter's box in St. Louis has been a long and painful road, one he took the first steps of all the way back in February.

## *MONSTER* mInutiae

Taken as the seventh pick overall in the draft, Nixon was only the second position player taken in the 1993 amateur draft (the first, and the first overall pick, was a shortstop out of Miami named Alex Rodriguez) and has turned out to be one of the rare high draft picks whose production at the major league level reached the level of expectations set for him by the organization.

## This Is the Year

Nixon's road to St. Louis began outside his home in Wilmington, North Carolina, in late February when he packed up his bats and began the drive down to the Sox' spring facility in Fort Myers, Florida. We like to imagine his thoughts on this drive drifting to the season ahead, to the excitement and anticipation that has been building around this team and this season since its last game the previous October, and to the role he will play in it all. Despite missing 28 games in 2003, most of them near the end of the season, Nixon is coming off easily the best season of his career, establishing highs in batting average and home runs, and the steady upward trajectory of his previous three seasons promises that 2004 will likely be even better. He will play right field and hit either sixth or seventh, comfortable in nearly the same record-breaking lineup that took the field the year before. He will play behind better pitching. He will play behind a better closer. He will face a Yankee team without a left-handed starter 19 times over the course of the season. He will hit .300 again, establish himself as a .300-hitter; and he will hit the 30 home run, 100 RBI plateau he would have surely reached without the late injury in '03 (he finished with 28 HRs and 87 RBI). He may even make his first All-Star team.

All these wonderful things will happen for Trot, so long as he stays healthy. But then somewhere along this drive to Florida, perhaps during these very thoughts, Nixon's back begins to tighten, uncomfortably so, and by the time he reaches Ft. Myers, the discomfort in his back has become painful, and he likely knows it the moment he steps from the car: Something is wrong.

## Left Behind

What was wrong was a disc in Nixon's back that had, somewhere along the twelve-hour drive from winter to spring, become slightly herniated. He was immediately listed as day-to-day, then questionable for the start of the season, then definitely out of the Opening Day lineup, then out for all of spring training, and suddenly Trot Nixon, before he even unpacked his bats, was looking at a return sometime during the warm, mid-summer days of early June. At best.

As the team went through its lazy spring training schedule, through light workouts and casual, smiling, feet-up interviews where they talked of the excitement of Opening Day and the outlook for the season, Trot began rehab. And when the team packed up and headed to Baltimore, he stayed behind in Florida, his drive down having made it impossible for him to leave. He began a monotonous rehab process which, because of the nature of the injury, involved more waiting than work.

We picture him there, in a suddenly quiet and sleepy Florida town, walking into a nearly empty bar, shuffling up with the same deliberate, slightly pigeon-toed walk, giving a slight wince as he props himself up on a stool and motions to the bartender. He orders a beer, orders some dinner, and pulls his hat down a bit as the Sox game begins on the television above the bar.

## *MONSTER* minutiae

As odd as it seems, a scene very similar to this actually did take place—a rehabbing Nixon walked into a bar (full of Sox fans watching the game) and quietly ate dinner and watched the game. No one recognized him. This is perhaps understandable given Trot's generally blue collar, everyman look, but it also may have to do with the fact that at that moment, Trot Nixon was simply not on the minds of Red Sox fans, who were busy worrying about Pedro's first start and who would play both right field and shortstop.

## No. 7

Eleven years before Trot Nixon sat down at a bar in Florida to watch the Sox play on television, he was drafted out of high school as the

Red Sox first pick in the 1993 amateur draft, making him only one of two players on the 2004 Sox who were drafted into their minor league system (the other is rookie Kevin Youkilis), and the oldest tenured player within the organization, by far.

## CURSE BUSTERS

Since Nixon arrived in 1993, the Red Sox have: gone through three GMs; changed managers five times; changed ownership once; seen Clemens, Boggs, and Gordon leave (and go to the Yankees); seen Pedro, Varitek, and Manny arrive (and have seen Jeff Suppan arrive, leave, arrive again, and leave again); made the postseason four times and finished second to the Yankees six times (and watched them win four championships). In that time, Fenway Park has added: seats behind the roof boxes; two rows of seats behind home plate; seats on top of the left field wall; seats on the right field terrace; and even new restrooms. And over all that time, the only constants seem to be the blue hats, the scarlet "B", and No. 7, Trot Nixon.

He made his major league debut for the Red Sox at the end of the 1996 season (he went 2-4 with a double in two games). At the time, the only member of the eventual World Series winning team in the Sox clubhouse was a thin knuckleballer named Tim Wakefield, making Nixon the second piece in the championship puzzle and making Nixon and Wake the first of its teammates. In 1999, he arrived at spring training, made the Opening Day roster, and has been with the Red Sox ever since, gradually working into the everyday right field position that he took over during the 2001 season and has held ever since.

## A Mudder

But more so than even the time spent under the Red Sox hat itself, Nixon has defined himself as a Red Sox through his play on the field. Dust-covered and sweaty, with pine tar caked on his helmet and chalk covering his hat, Nixon is the kind of player with dirt under his fingernails and unaccountable cuts and bruises on his arms. He plays the game as if he is prepared at any moment, should the game suddenly require it of him, to tackle someone. A typical Nixon at-bat ends with him pulling himself up from a cloud of dust and sweeping dirt off his knees and chest, then pulling his helmet off and wiping the sweat from his forehead with the inside of his elbow brace. A typical Nixon catch ends with him pulling chunks of grass out of his belt, and examining his elbow as he runs off the field, presumably to make sure it's still in one piece. Of course, this type of gritty, meat-and-potatoes play amounts to flirting when it comes to the fans in Fenway's bleachers, and the love affair between Red Sox fans and Trot has been as complete and amicable as any at Fenway.

## *MONSTER* minutiae

The '04 Red Sox might not be the prettiest of groups—they're certainly not the best-groomed team in the league—but they will whoop your ass. All they need is a reason (as A-Rod and the Yankees found out). Top to bottom, their roster is loaded with guys you would want behind you—or better yet, in front of you—in a street fight; chief among them being Varitek (obviously), but also Ortiz, Millar, Kapler, Timlin, Embree, and Nixon, who may not even need a reason.

And this is what must have made life in the empty batting cages and sleepy bars of Fort Myers so miserable for Nixon throughout most of the summer, to sit there where you do not belong, watching the silent scenes of your teammates in the field, of your ballpark and your fans, watching the Sox battle out a close game in the afternoon sun at Fenway, pushing away an empty plate and taking a pull from a warm beer, waiting.

# Back in Action

Eventually Nixon's back healed, he regained flexibility, and the pain began to go away. But in one of his rehab games in Florida, he felt something in his left quad, a tweak, a slight pain that intensified when he ran the bases or ranged through the outfield, and suddenly, just as one injury healed, his rehabbing a slightly herniated disc dovetailed into his rehabbing a slightly strained quad. The new injury pushed his timetable back even farther, until the middle of June, when he finally rejoined his teammates on the road and began his 2004 season on June 16th in Colorado.

He hit a home run, pulling a 1-1 breaking ball into the right field stands in just his second at-bat of the season. Trot was back. He made his first start at Fenway on June 22nd against the Twins, and with Nomar Garciaparra back in the lineup that same night (he hit a grand slam in the seventh), Terry Francona finally wrote out the lineup every Sox fan had waited all winter and most of the summer to see.

As for Nixon, the season was still fat with potential—almost 100 games remained, plus the postseason, and with the Sox still in the chase for the AL East, there would be big games ahead, long drawn-out battles deep into the night, filled with desperately slim leads and improbable rallies. And Nixon would be in the middle of it all, coming up with men on and the Sox down, ranging through the Fenway outfield, barreling into the bullpen wall, sliding across the thick summer grass. All this was still there for Trot, stretching out across the long late-summer months, waiting for him.

## . . . And Back in Inaction

He played 29 games. Then, the day after the Sox epic 11-10 win over the Yankees, Nixon was out of the lineup due to a flare-up in his sore left quad. Later, he was re-examined, and it was revealed that the injury had worsened, and that it would continue to worsen the longer he played on it. He went back on the DL at the end of July—back to rehab, back to waiting. This time, though, the circumstances were much darker for Nixon; the entire season was now in question. The nature of the injury (the depth of the strain) would not guarantee a full recovery by the end of the season, and even a full recovery would not guarantee his effectiveness once he came back. There were serious doubts about his ability to help the team win if he came back to the lineup, and even more serious doubts about the likelihood of his returning to the lineup at all. The fans were advised, through so many means, to prepare to go the rest of the season without seeing No. 7 in the lineup.

And so Trot Nixon entered into his own version of baseball purgatory: Since he could not rule out a return, he would have to work as hard as he had ever worked to rehab for a possible comeback, but the nature of his injury meant all this work would likely be done in vain.

A crueler, more trying situation could hardly be imagined for a player defined as a gamer, competing hard every inning of every game of every season. To not be able to compete, to not be able to help his teammates, must have been torture. How many times must he have been asked, *how you feelin', Trot?* or, *how's the leg, Trot?* How many times must he have been interviewed about being able to return, or about not being able to return? How many times must he have wondered, late at night, whether there would be any baseball left for him before spring of '05? How many times must he have thought about coming up to the plate, in a big game, in the World Series, with runners on; and how many times must he have thought about sitting on the bench, leg wrapped, watching?

Through it all, he did all that he could do: He prayed, worked, and waited. Meanwhile, the Sox began to pick things up in mid-August, reeling off a series of wins and making the AL East race interesting for the first time in months. There were new faces to see, new names to pronounce, and new stories to hear; and during all this time Trot Nixon remained a shadowy presence in the background, nearly forgotten, but not quite.

We imagine these as Trot's own thoughts, focusing all of his work and energy on a point somewhere in October, thinking of that one at-bat in a key situation. Should he be able to step up to the plate in that situation, even if it were his only at-bat of the entire season, all the work and all the doubt and all the waiting would be instantly justified—it would have all been worth it, after all. And if not—if the healing process dragged on, and the leg did not get better, and his whole summer of hard work and sweat and waiting went for nothing at all—then he would at the very least be spared the guilt of wondering whether he had worked hard enough or not. The answers to these questions were never in doubt with Nixon, the effort would always be there and the work would always be done, those facts he knew; they were, at the time, the only thing he could be certain of at all.

## End of the Road

Trot Nixon steps into the batter's box in Busch Stadium and takes his stance, his feet spread wide in the box, knees bent and body leaning slightly back over his left foot, the majority of his weight held up by his thick left leg. He bobs back, yanks the handle of the bat above his back shoulder with a quick jerk, then settles it down a bit and gradually rocks it, waving the end high in the air, and looks out to the mound.

On the rubber, Jason Marquis—now facing the bases loaded with two outs in a one-run elimination game, in the World Series—still does not look as nervous as perhaps he should be (which is bound to make Cardinals fans even more nervous than they already are). Taking his sign, he comes set on the rubber, then fires a fastball near the dirt and off the outside edge of the plate for ball one. He gets the ball back from his catcher, steps back to the mound, and even though Jason Marquis and Trot Nixon have never faced each other, both understand each other's circumstance and perspective.

Marquis has shown that he knows the scouting report on Nixon, which is to keep the ball down, way down; he would like to force Nixon to chase something low and chop an easy grounder to an infielder. Nixon, on the other hand, knows that Marquis does not want to walk him, but also knows that the last thing Marquis wants to do is give up a big hit, and so he will not be taking any chances by challenging Nixon with a pitch to hit. Both assumptions are validated by the first ball low and away, and both are confirmed by Marquis's second pitch, also a ball, also low. The third pitch is even lower, running the count to 3-0.

# *MONSTER* minutiae

Nixon's swing, while flexible and able to adjust to a number of pitches, is more or less designed to take balls up in the zone and slightly out over the plate and pull them very hard and very deep into the seats in right to right-center field. He does this primarily by getting down low on his back leg, keeping his front hip in, and exploding both up and out when he pulls his bat up through the zone at a slight angle, lifting the ball up and, hopefully, out.

Nixon steps out of the box and looks down the third base line. He secures his helmet, grabs the bat, steps back in the box, takes his stance, raises his bat, and at this exact point in time, reaches the moment he has prayed for, and worked for, and waited for all spring and all summer long, through all the drills and all the exercises, through all the examinations and all the prognoses, during all the interviews and all the questions (*what do ya think Trot, you comin' back?*), and among every quiet moment of hope and doubt and worry along the way. The promise of a moment like this—World Series, Game Four, 3rd inning, Sox ahead a run, bases loaded, two outs, 3-0 count, Nixon at bat—ran quietly beneath them all.

It is the end of many long roads for Trot Nixon, and they all end right at this instant in St. Louis when Jason Marquis unwinds and throws and Trot Nixon does all he ever wanted to do from the moment he began driving away from his home in Wilmington—he drops down on his back leg, drops his hands, drives off his back side, pulls the bat handle into the zone and explodes through the ball, driving it deep out into the night air above right-center field. The ball rockets out into the gap, high up, and as Nixon rounds first and Ortiz scores from third it falls and clips the top edge of the wall just below its yellow rim. Manny scores from second, giving the Sox a 3-0 lead, and Nixon pulls up into second with a two-out, two-run double.

Three months after he went back on the DL with a season-ending injury, eight months after he left his home to drive to Florida, and eleven years after the Sox made him their first pick in the 1993 draft, Trot Nixon is exactly where he is supposed to be—dusting himself off on second, having just launched a two-run double. The Sox are now comfortably leading the game and are six short innings away from winning the World Series. And this, of course, was always how it was supposed to be; this was always where Trot Nixon, like his Red Sox teammates and the fans who followed them, was supposed be in the very end—it was only a matter of time, only a matter of how much work, only a matter of how long and how difficult the road.

**idiot RULE:** *When in doubt, fly there.*

# Mr. Good Time Rally Cowboy-UP Guy

**For the majority** of Kevin Millar's first two seasons with the Red Sox he has behaved like a man who is just happy to be here; more specifically, he has behaved like a man who is just happy to *not* be in Japan. After signing with the Chunichi Dragons in the winter of 2002–03, Millar began to have second thoughts, then quickly decided against the idea. He was less quickly extricated from his contract, and even less quickly maneuvered—through a complex set of negotiations orchestrated by then-rookie GM Theo Epstein—to the Red Sox. (Incidentally, there is perhaps no player on this Red Sox team and few players anywhere who would appear to be a worse fit for Japanese culture than Kevin Millar—the comic potential of the fit seemingly better suited for bad sitcom than baseball.) Since then he has bounced into Fenway more or less every day with more or less the same ornery half-grin, the same comfortable step, the same alert, expectant look on his face which seems to say, upon climbing the dugout steps to batting practice, *Hey-hey, how 'bout this; this is alright, huh?*

## First Impressions

We find him there now, during a lazy midsummer batting practice, doing what we are most likely to find him doing: talking. Because we are at Fenway, and because we are mercifully left alone to simply sit in an empty ballpark and observe, we find him talking not with a microphone in his face but to a teammate (say, Ortiz). The two stand on a sunny patch of outfield grass just beyond first base, Ortiz upright and leaning on a bat and smiling wide as he watches the hitters relay in and out of the cage; Millar at his side, talking. He is of average height and slightly above-average weight and hardly cuts a striking figure (particularly standing there next to Papi). His barrel-chested physique has often earned him the appellation of being something of a throwback, a vintage-style ballplayer who reminds us of baseball's golden age and golden heroes—which is all a rather polite way of noting that he does not appear to have taken advantage of the many modern advances in fitness or nutrition that are available to today's athletes.

Adding to this throwback look are the red socks, pulled knee-high, and the thick growth of hair on his chin surrounded by a three-day stubble across his jaw (although this particular aspect of Millar, above anything, is prone to change throughout the season).

## *MONSTER* minutiae

At various times throughout his first two seasons, Millar has gone with: the full goatee, the full beard, the half-goatee/thin-beard, the no-beard/soul patch, the Civil War era ultra-goatee, the fu-manchu, the fu-manchu/semi-beard, the thin jawline-only beard, the complicated thin jawline-only beard into fu-manchu combination, the basic retro goatee, and countless others. And that's not to mention his complimentarily array of hairstyles, the most notable of which was an unfortunate dye job known to Sox fans as Millar's "human tennis ball" phase.

It is hard to tell, from our seat in the low first base grandstands, what exactly he is talking about (we get the impression that Kevin Millar knows more than a few good dirty jokes), but Ortiz has a wide grin across his face, and Millar smiles as he talks and gestures with his hands (flat-palmed and giving directions, movement). He begins to laugh, at one point slapping Papi's shoulder, then doubles over with a hand on his belly as Ortiz shakes his head and covers his face with his hand, pushing the still doubled-over Millar away in jest, the laughter floating back among the empty seats.

The overall impression we get as Millar wraps an arm around Ortiz's shoulder and gestures with his index finger to finish his story (whatever tale he has told Papi seems to contain something of a moral to it, an instructive epilogue) is of a man who thoroughly enjoys the moment and what he is doing, regardless of *what* he may be doing at any given moment. He might be giving an interview in the dugout, stepping into the batting cage, or talking to reporters outside his locker after a game, or throwing infield grounders between innings—all the mundane everyday duties in the routine of a major league baseball player that seem quickly to grow stale and tiresome for so many. Millar appears to relish each, and relish each consistently. Perhaps because of his last-minute escape from exile (*Hey man, I'm just glad I'm not in Japan*), or because of his less-than-athletic (*ehem*, throwback) physique, or his not-exactly-obvious baseball qualifications (more on that in a moment), Millar goes through every day of his professional life in the majors exactly how so many fans believe every player should—with a deep and powerful appreciation of how lucky he is to be a ballplayer, how fortunate he is to be on a big league roster, and how nice it is to stand on the outfield grass, in the sun, and play baseball.

Over the course of a season so much time is spent by fans and media holding a mirror up to the overpaid and underappreciative within the game, trying to impress these realizations upon them, and yet not nearly enough credit is given to the rare player like Millar who, without prompting, so freely emulates the way most fans imagine they too would react (that is: with laughter, smiles) if allowed to pull on a big league jersey and run out onto the Fenway grass on a warm summer evening. No one needs to tell Kevin Millar how astronomical the odds of his being here are; no one needs to explain to him how few the opportunities in life are to hear 35,000 people chanting your name; no one needs to remind him that he is being paid an absurd amount of money to play the game he loves. He knows. We hear this in his words and see this in the way he carries himself. While at times he will show his displeasure with a situation, and at times he will voice a complaint, at no time can anyone say that Kevin Millar has taken any of this for granted.

## Who Invited Millar?

It would be a disservice to the man to assume that his quick laugh and deep, easy enjoyment of life stem only from his enviable position as a professional athlete. It is an easy assumption to make, surely, but one that does not quite fit—not when one realizes how many athletes live similar lives and seem so dissimilarly unable to enjoy them. The way they carry themselves seems to be more a reflection of character than circumstance. We could easily imagine Kevin Millar with the same smile on his face, taking the same deep, easy enjoyment of life even if he was just our downstairs neighbor, our coworker at the plant, or our cousin's girlfriend's brother. And whether he was the Kevin who we went to junior high with or Millar, the Red Sox first baseman, we imagine that either way he would be a good guy to have around the barbeque. We can picture him holding a beer in one hand and slapping our Uncle Sal on the shoulders, doubling up in laughter with a hand on his belly, just as easily as we see him out there on the lip of the outfield grass, with his hand on Ortiz's shoulder and a smile on his face.

All of which at times may distract us from the reason Millar is in Boston to begin with, which is not because he enjoys life and keeps up the mood in the clubhouse but because he is a damn good baseball player. Somehow this tends to get lost, and understandably so.

He certainly does not physically look like an athlete, and most of the time he does not physically move like one, either. He does not run particularly fast; is not particularly strong; does not have a particularly great arm; and although he is not exactly clumsy, neither does he move with what can be described as effortless grace. As he once jokingly described himself: While other players bring certain tools to their game, he barely even has a toolbox. But this is not exactly true, either. What Millar does have is great hands—agile, soft, and dexterous—and, like all professional-caliber baseball players, he possesses astonishingly quick hand-eye reflexes. It is hard to think of someone with Millar's blue-collar sensibilities as being world class at anything, but the fact is that his mere presence on a Major League roster tells us that when it comes to hitting a baseball, Millar is among extremely elite company.

## The Duel

His bat speed alone is evidence of this world-class skill, and one of the singular pleasures of watching Millar's game comes when he faces a somewhat cocky, somewhat stubborn flamethrower who tries to throw a fastball by the big-swinging righty. He tries one and Millar, who absolutely lives on hitting fastballs, takes a big cut only to foul it off, the force of his swing carrying him out over the plate. He steps back over, sweeps a pile of dirt across the box with the inside of his foot and leans over and spits, then grabs the handle of the bat with both hands and twists the pine tar over its handle as he looks out to the mound. (*Alright partner, you wanna go; let's go.*)

He plants his right foot in the back of the box, digs in, and brings his left foot down in front and out to the side, opening his hips and shoulders to the mound as he faces out. He holds the bat back above his right shoulder and waves its head down in quick jabs toward the pitcher. The quicker the waves, the more amped up he is to jump on the fastball; the more amped up he is, the more he challenges the pitcher to throw it; and the more he challenges the pitcher to throw it, the more likely it is to be thrown and the more we lean in at this most basic of one-on-one baseball moments—one man trying to throw a baseball as hard as he can and another man trying to hit it.

Fenway, sensing the moment (*come on, Millah!*), comes to life; the bat waves quicker. If the pitcher is smart, mature, and a good crafts-man, he will throw a breaking ball in the dirt here and Millar will swing himself sideways trying to hit a baseball that is no longer there. More than likely, however, the pitcher is immature and cocky and will attempt to throw the hardest fastball in the history of organized base-ball, and Millar will either yank it hard foul, a whistling missile back into the seats that sends fans diving for cover, or time it just right and scorch it to the outfield wall, perhaps even beyond. Either way, the pleasure of the situation exists for the fans (and for the players, too, we assume) in the moment just before the pitcher is set to deliver, when he and Millar and all the rest of us know exactly what is coming, and we all draw in a bit closer to watch the challenge.

## The Ballplayer

But more so than even his bat speed, what Kevin Millar has are instincts. He is a classic example of the difference between an athlete and a ballplayer who understands the game of baseball on an intuitive level. The game just makes sense to Millar. Some of this understanding comes simply from a lifetime of playing the game, of living on a baseball field, but then there are many others even at this high level who have lived the game their entire lives and still look lost within it. They know how to hit, how to catch, and how to throw, but they do not yet (and may never) *know* how to play baseball. This is abstract, unscientific stuff, of course, but then those around the game know that the best way of understanding this distinction is by being at the ballpark and watching the game itself. Because when we do, we see that the game is made up of many different types of men. It has its strong men and its tall men, its fast men and its agile men, its acrobatic men and its muscle men. Kevin Millar is one of the many who is both less than and more than all of these. He is a baseball man.

## Millar, On the Record

Now that he is a baseball man in Boston, he is also a man whose actions are consistently followed by a gallery of cameras, and whose words are consistently recorded by a bouquet of microphones. This can be either good or bad for someone like Kevin Millar. Good when it captures his humor and energy and enthusiasm, bad when it captures errant thoughts that come to him as he speaks—thoughts that will be recorded and printed and later discussed at length on drive-time radio.

There have been many instances of the former (hundreds), and yet the latter moments still stand out, none more so than the now famous monologue Millar delivered in the clubhouse on August 19, 2003. It was the day after a particularly crushing Sox loss to Oakland, and right in the middle of a particularly muggy and uncomfortable patch of the summer for both the Sox and their fans. When asked about the general atmosphere surrounding the ballclub at the time, Millar was quoted (by Bob Hohler in the *Globe* the following day) as saying: "I want to see somebody cowboy up and stand behind this team one time and quit worrying about all the negative stuff and talking about last year's team and 10 years ago and 1986. I don't know better, man. I'm here to win and have fun. [The past] makes no sense to me."

# MONSTER minutiae

It almost goes without saying that Millar has, among other things, been a good fit for the native tongue of his adopted city, and in his first year was a part of the All-Time Boston Accent Infield of: Mill*ah*, Walk*ah*, Nom*ah*, and Muell*ah*.

Unfortunately, to the eventual chagrin of Sox fans everywhere and the delight of retailers throughout New England, the part of this statement that the media picked up on was the peculiar but rather insignificant phrase *cowboy up*. And through the storm of T-shirts and signs and commemorative merchandise that followed in the wake of its publication, what Millar actually *said* became lost. Regrettably so, since it is perhaps the single most succinct declaration of what Kevin Millar really brought to the Sox clubhouse, and why he was ultimately so instrumental in the team's eventual, historic success.

It is consistent with what Johnny Damon would later dub the idiot-mentality of his teammates that Kevin Millar's most telling quote in a Red Sox uniform would be the simple head-shaking confusion that caused him to mutter, *Makes no sense to me*. And contrary to what the *Globe* implied (by making "[The past]" his subject) what really made no sense to Millar was not the past itself, but the preoccupation with it, expressed so relentlessly and so unabashedly by so many Sox fans for so long. What sent Millar off on his famous rant was the continual digging up of past mistakes made by past players on past teams, and the implication that somehow all of this should matter to the men in the present clubhouse. It made no sense, no sense at all.

## A Case of Voluntary Amnesia

This obsession with the past made no sense to Millar and fortunately not for many others in the Red Sox dugout, either—revealing one of the key elements that has made his generation of Sox teams so successful, and so very different from Sox teams of the past: namely, an ability to focus on the day at hand, and to really, truly, completely live free of the burdens of history. In a broad sense, this meant refusing to talk or debate or (more importantly) even think about anything that happened to the Sox over the previous 86 seasons. But in a much more practical and significant sense, it meant forgetting about what happened to the Sox the previous night. Given the tremendous weight of the former we might assume that unshackling it was the more difficult of tasks, but this was not necessarily so. Most of the Red Sox players were not around for much of the last 86 years, living and dying with the Red Sox, so a general lack of knowledge may have lightened the unloading of this baggage; but they *had* lived through the night before; and the week before; and, for many, the year before. These memories were somewhat more vivid than *10 years ago* or

*1986*, and the fact that Millar and his teammates were able to forget about these fresher, more lively ghosts is one of the truest marks of their collective character, and the truest mark by far of Millar's influence with their clubhouse. And at no point was this mark clearer or more significant than on the night of October 17, 2004, in the fading evening hours leading up to Game Four of the ALCS.

Earlier in the week, fans had witnessed one of the more ominous scenes of the season after the Sox dropped Game Two of the series in New York. On their televisions, they saw Kevin Millar alone on the Red Sox bench, seated in full uniform and surrounded only by a scattering of paper cups, hands on knees, and head down. (He had struck out against Mariano Rivera to end the game, swinging through a high fastball—a pitch he would see again, later on.) It is one thing to witness your team go down in defeat, but quite another to see its spirit broken—particularly when that spirit comes in the form of a man who had so far been defined by his unbreakable spirit and optimism—and this image of Millar Defeated was not one many Sox fans were prepared, or able, to process.

We were no less prepared and no less able to process what happened two nights later in Game Three when the Sox were again defeated and perhaps many more spirits were broken; but the significant moment for Millar and the Sox came shortly after, at the most unlikely of all times, during batting practice before Game Four. It was at this time, as Peter Gammons would later report on-air, that Kevin Millar took to bouncing around, telling anyone who would listen, *Don't let us win this game, Don't let us win this game.* Hardly menacing advice to the players and media who had recently watched the Yankees, without being told, quite effortlessly *not* let Boston win anything. But Millar stood by the soundness of his advice: *We win this one, then we got Pedro and Schilling, and then anything can happen in a Game Seven.*

This is, of course, selective amnesia on an absurd level; but it worked. The Sox forgot all about Games 1–3 and even innings 1–8 of the current game, and as they entered the ninth down a run and down to (possibly) their final three outs of the season, they sent the right man up to the plate to lead things off. No. 15 stepped to the plate. For all Kevin Millar has said and done in his first two years in Boston, it is somehow ironic that one of his biggest contributions to their eventual championship was made by not doing anything—specifically, by *not* swinging the bat. Facing Rivera again, Millar yanked the second pitch he saw foul, but managed to lay off the first, inside, and the following three, all inside and the last one high around his chin. He drew the walk, and instead of forgetting history, Kevin Millar helped make it.

# *MONSTER* minutiae

It is surprising to note that although we tend to think of him as being a big guy (perhaps from the size of his personality and swing), Millar is basically human-sized. For comparison, he is listed at the exact same height and weight (6′, 210 pounds) as Keith Foulke.

Three nights later, as he celebrated with his teammates on the field at Yankee Stadium (looking out at the same dugout he had hung his head in a week earlier), he was not looking ahead to the World

Series, and was not looking back at the season or the playoffs or even the recently completed series. He was celebrating that night and that achievement, and as he threw his arm around reporters and hugged his teammates, laughing and smiling as we had watched him do every day for two summers, there was a sense that Kevin Millar, of all the people involved in the celebration, was once again taking nothing for granted. In fact, he looked very much like a man who was just happy to be there.

**idiot RULE:** *Quit worrying about the negative stuff.*

# Chapter 7

# The Quiet Ones

## Billy at the Bat

**Bill Mueller** speaks in clichés. He says things like, *I'm
just trying to do the best I
can*, and, *I'm just one of
twenty-five guys who've
got a common goal*, and,
more frequently, *I was just
fortunate*. We have heard this
all before; it is playerspeak—the
tired lines and well-worn epitaphs
that appear in every sports page, in
every paper, every day. As fans we
read past them almost instinctively as

background noise. And this, of course, is because clichés are dead phrases—their original meanings dried up from overuse and incapable (from exhaustion) of bringing us any closer to understanding.

Professional baseball players (and professional baseball players in Boston, in particular), spend an absurd amount of time facing cameras and microphones over the course of a 162-game season (not to mention a thirty-game preseason and a fourteen-game postseason), in front of which they answer questions before each game and after each game; not to mention the dozens of small, ten-second encounters between the postgame interviews' end and the following pregame interviews commencement; and, quite obviously, there simply is not enough to say.

This, then, is one of the reasons players tend to repeat the same phrases over and over, simply because they have to say something—there is a microphone in their face. (Of course, as most players point out, they are also asked the same questions—*how did it feel to hit the game-winning home run?; how do you feel about being in a slump?*—over and over again.) So for two weeks they say things like, *I'm just glad I could help the team win* and *I'm just trying to take it one day at a time.*

Occasionally, however, our familiarity with these petrified phrases will cause us to read past them too quickly, and by doing so miss something significant in either the speaker or his subject. This, it seems, is the case with Bill Mueller.

## Like a Broken Record

Over time, one of the differences we notice between the cliché-use of Mueller and that of his peers is that while all athletes use clichés (some occasionally, some frequently), Bill Mueller uses them relentlessly. In every interview, one after another. This becomes almost comical at a certain point. After all, it isn't easy to use four or five clichés in a row, back-to-back-to-back. Try it sometime. Chances are, an original or vivid phrase will sneak in there eventually, just by accident.

And although most athletes break from their clichés at some point, when a particular game or (more likely) a particularly tactless question inspires them to do so, Mueller never does. Throughout the season and throughout each interview, his cliché use remains consistent, unfailing, and repetitively repetitive.

It is worth pointing out here, too, that one of the reasons many athletes use clichés is the same reason many of the rest of us do, which is a simple lack of articulation. They, like the rest of us, often want to express a deeper, more vivid emotion or reaction to the events around them, but simply cannot put the words together to do so. We all do this—it's like riding a bike and it happens to the best of us, day in and day out, until the cows come home. For many athletes, clichés become a way of getting around these problems with articulation, and allow them to communicate with their fans despite these obstacles.

This is not, however, the case with Bill Mueller, who is quite articulate, who speaks clearly and without hesitation, and in whose hushed, concentrated voice is the sound of someone who is concerned with being understood. It is the voice of someone who cares about your understanding—the voice of a kindergarten teacher. Ironically, it is the consistent repetition of these clichés—themselves the product of repetition—that hints to us that something else is going on with how Bill Mueller uses them.

While the baseball season can be, at times, repetitive, it is hardly ever consistent (and even less so when the Red Sox are involved). The spikes of optimism and enthusiasm combined with the various plummets of misfortune and bitter gloom make a break from the consistent comforts of everyday clichés almost an inevitability. At some point, we assume, the sheer emotion of the moment, either positive or negative, would inspire even the most unimaginative speaker to break form and offer some colorful insight into the complexities of the situation.

And yet, as we follow Bill Mueller through his first two seasons in Boston (he signed as a free agent in January '03), we continue to see him reach these heights and (less often) depths, and we continue to hear the same reactions.

We continue to learn that he *is just trying to do the best he can*, even as he, oh, let's see, hits a grand slam one night in Texas and then, oh well, hits another one the very next inning from the other side of the plate. The announcers tell us that this has never been done in the history of the game, and oh hey look, there are Billy Mueller's batting gloves in the Hall of Fame (huh, that's neat; he certainly was trying his best that night, huh). And there's his name over there, too, on that shiny bat on the wall and, let's have a look then, it says here that in 2003 Billy Mueller was the American League Batting Champion, huh, that's pretty neat, too. Even as these remarkable achievements and awards and honors have come to Mueller, his response has stayed the same as it was the first day of training. *I was just trying to do the best I can*, he says, and when pressed will only add, *I was fortunate.*

# Out of the Spotlight

There is one instance though, and one instance only, when Bill Mueller breaks from his script about playing hard and helping the team, etcetera. This one instance when Mueller suddenly speaks openly and enthusiastically, and often at length, allows us the brief glimpse we need to see into his reason for using so many clichés in the first place. This one instance comes not when the game or moment is heightened, but when the subject is shifted from Bill Mueller to any one of his teammates.

Here, for example, is Bill Mueller when asked about Bill Mueller: "There are so many things I could be better with. This game is an exercise in constantly improving not only year after year but at-bat after at-bat" (from the *Boston Globe*, April 16, 2004).

Here is Bill Mueller on teammate Pedro Martinez: ". . . any time a type of player like Pedro is on the mound, I have a ton of confidence in Pedro because he's a special pitcher . . . That guy competes as hard as anybody, and, you know, I'm very fortunate to be able to play behind him because I know playing against him was very difficult, and I like my situation where I'm behind him and supporting him rather than facing him, believe me. He's an excellent pitcher" (from *www.mlb.com*, October 18, 2004).

Over the course of the season, as we hear similar contrasts repeated into a distinct patter, we begin to realize what we might have suspected all along: Mueller's clichés come not from a lack of originality or creativity or even awareness—we can see in his comments on others how acutely he understands his environment—but rather from a genuine, all-encompassing humility.

# A Face in the Crowd

Humility in star athletes, whose lives and livelihoods seemed designed to remind them of the fact that they have little to be humble about, is always a problematic subject, particularly so when said athlete is the one informing us of said humility. (As in, *I'm humble.* [*Sure you are.*] *No, really, I am—stand here and listen to me talk about how humble I am for an hour and I'll prove it to you.*)

The difference between Bill Mueller and so many others for whom statements of humility become another way of drawing admiration to themselves is that we do not learn of his humility through his words so much as through his actions. He simply lives it. The fan who follows him throughout the season realizes this, but only over time. (Humility is a hard trait to observe, but then, that's the point.)

Nothing Bill Mueller does is designed to draw attention to himself. Quite the opposite, in fact—most of his actions and every last one of his words seem designed to deflect attention away from him, sending it back into the clubhouse and onto his teammates, more than a few of whom are quite comfortable in the spotlight.

At average height (5'10") and weight (180 lbs), Mueller does not physically stand out. His perpetually wide-open eyes and disarming Midwestern features suggest a face in the crowd (perhaps a kindergarten teacher from Missouri, visiting Fenway on vacation). And on a team that has been defined, and at times has defined itself, by its expressively individual hairstylings, Mueller has stuck with the buzz cut and a trim, graying goatee.

Standing in the back row of the Red Sox' otherwise Sergeant Pepperian team photo, he just looks like a guy. Just a guy in the back.

And just a guy on the bench during the game, a guy who high-fives his teammates when they enter the dugout after scoring and congratulates the departing pitchers on the top step. Otherwise, he sits on the bench and watches the game and chats with his teammates.

*MONSTER* minutiae

Mueller did not grow out his goatee much before coming to Boston, but grew it in early in the 2003 season. Around midsummer, after a scorching start at the plate, Mueller went clean-shaven (during which the thirty-two-year-old could have passed for around twenty) and immediately went into the only extended slump of his batting title season. The goatee was back a week later, Mueller broke out of the slump, and has not been clean-shaven since.

He is not on the top step dancing; he is not pointing at the dugout camera; he is not looking back over the dugout talking to fans; and he does not have a dance. What you see when you notice Bill Mueller (if you notice him at all, which you certainly might not) is what is left standing when everything else about him—the way he looks, or the way he acts, or what he says—becomes opaque. It just so happens that this is exactly what we bought our ticket to see in the first place, which is how Bill Mueller plays baseball.

## Doing the Little Things Right

Ironically enough, the first thing we learn when we focus on how he plays the game of baseball is that Mueller actually has a great deal to be proud of. Although he does not dominate any one area of the game,

Mueller is above average in nearly all of them. At third, he combines inch-perfect reflexes with soft hands and a solid, accurate arm. He commands third base with a veteran's deep-rooted baseball instincts.

These same instincts serve him well in the finer points of the game—the details, the basics. These are the areas not often mentioned in highlight reels or history books, but which distinguish one nondescript player from another and, often enough, distinguish one competitive team from another.

Mueller does them all well. He runs the bases intelligently. He throws to the right base in the right situation. He knows how to slide (not as common among big leaguer players as you might imagine); and he is one of the few Red Sox players who can be trusted to lay down a bunt (ditto).

There is nothing on a baseball field that Bill Mueller does poorly, and because of this, he has earned the label of being a throwback. Recently, it's become somewhat fashionable to label any player who pulls up his stockings knee-high, as Mueller does, and runs out every ground ball hard a throwback, but it is rarely accurate. In fact, there are only two real throwbacks on this Red Sox team, and Mueller is one of them (Trot Nixon is the other). And he can flat-out hit. The batting title alone should be enough evidence of this, but should we require more evidence, we need only watch the man swing the bat.

## Like Riding a Bike

He steps to the plate now on the left side, facing a right-handed pitcher. With red stockings pulled knee-high and red sleeves reaching down to his white Franklin batting gloves (circa 1987, speaking of throwbacks), he takes his stance directly, without embellishment. No waving the bat three times or spitting on his gloves or adjusting his helmet. He simply steps in and faces the pitcher. He stands up on his toes, holds the bat back above and behind his shoulder, strums his fingers on the handle and, as the pitcher comes set, stretches his hands back even further. Square to the pitcher, he waits, bobs up higher on his toes, and stretches his hands back an inch further.

When the pitch is delivered (a difficult slider, low and a bit away) the front foot goes down and knees bend and the front shoulder stays closed as the head locks in and the hands follow, straight down, inside the ball. He whips the bat through the zone and twists his torso into the snapshot follow-through—the bat in his right hand and swung around to his back leg, the left hand pushing out, palm open, in front of the body, knees bent, head down but just now looking up to find the ball, eyes wide open.

By now, the ball is sailing out over the wide gap in left-center on a smooth low-hassle flight to the warning track, and as Mueller sprints up the line with his arms pumping and head leaning slightly back (as if there might be a close play at first) he gives a little glance back, over his left shoulder, to the runner rounding third and heading home—just to make sure—and by the time he has rounded first and pulled up easily on second for an RBI double we no longer question the fact that Bill Mueller can flat-out hit. The swing, without further argument or evidence, has made its own case.

It is a swing that over the last two seasons has impressed many, including most of the pitchers in the American League and every last one of his teammates—chief among them David Ortiz, who once called Mueller the best switch-hitter he'd ever seen, adding that he was *perfect from both sides of the plate.*

Perfect is an interesting choice of words. It is a word that Mueller, within all of his clichés, repeatedly uses (in contexts such as, *we're trying to be perfect every night,* and so on). Important enough to repeat, the word tells us something else about Mueller that we can assume to be true and at the same time assume that he is too humble to ever admit—his consistently high level of play represents not only great skill but great determination as well.

Bill Mueller is something of a perfectionist, and like all other perfectionists, we assume that he is far more troubled by his failures than pleased with triumphs. He simply sets the standard for himself too high for it to be otherwise, which is sad and at the same time extremely fortunate for Red Sox fans, who perhaps benefit most from Mueller's determination. We are the ones who are allowed to enjoy the perfect one-handed scoop up the line, the snap peg to first, the difficult inside-out single. We are the ones who ultimately cheer on the fact that Bill Mueller tries to be perfect every night—because on certain nights this season, he was.

## Tearing Up the Script

Each baseball season is threaded with its own peculiar ironic twists, and among the many choice ironies of this Red Sox season the choicest may be this: that on a team packed with eccentric stars, it was the humble guy, the guy who deflects attention and blends into the background, who ultimately came up with not only the biggest hit of the regular season, but the biggest hit of the postseason as well. That both hits came at

Fenway in the bottom of the ninth, with a man on and the Sox trailing by a run, and that both came off the man widely acknowledged as the greatest closer to ever play the game, only adds irony upon irony.

The first of these, the hit many Sox fans point to as the single most significant hit of the regular season, came on a windy evening at Fenway (July 24, 2004), at the tail end of a long, tense, brutally emotional game that saw a bit of everything. There were three lead changes, two ties, eleven pitchers, three ejections, one hit batsman, a half dozen or so four-letter words directed at the wrong catcher, and one of the most memorable images of this or any other seasons, followed by an old-fashioned mayhem-style bench-clearing brawl.

All of this happened before Bill Mueller stepped to the plate with one out in the bottom of the ninth, with Kevin Millar on first and the Sox down a run. With Mariano Rivera (the aforementioned greatest closer in the history of the game) uncharacteristically wild low in the zone, Mueller worked the count to 3-1 before Rivera elevated a pitch up and out over the plate (Mueller's pitch, a hitter's pitch). He drilled it on a line into deep right, still going back into the teeth of a strong wind, hanging as all of Fenway shouted and waved and Gary Sheffield drifted back, settled, and then stopped and looked up.

Fenway Park erupted—and for a few minutes, the world became a delirious blur of arms and hands and smiles and jubilant, deafening noise. By the time Fenway finally turned back over and settled upright again, the Sox had won and the Yankees had been beaten. Billy Mueller was in front of the Sox dugout with a headset on, shrugging as he told the television announcers, *I was just trying to put a good swing on it.*

# A Storybook Ending

The second hit, the one for the bedtime stories, came in a nearly identical situation to the first. However, it was significant not for what the hit ended, but what it kept from ending: namely, the Red Sox' season. Although we (if we are baseball fans of any stripe) have heard the story many times by now, we have yet to tire of its rhythms, and so we may tuck in tight, and hear it once again (with apologies, this time, to Ernest Lawrence Thayer).

*It was 17 October 2004,*
*and the outlook was far from brilliant for the Boston nine that night;*
*the score stood four to three with but one inning left to fight.*
*So upon that stricken multitude grim melancholy sat;*
*for there seemed but little chance of Billy's getting up to bat.*
*But Millar let by a trio, and the fourth was called a ball;*
*and Roberts, in to run, sprinted down to get the call.*
*And when the dust had lifted, and the fans saw what had occurred,*
*there was Roberts safe at second and the scoring chance assured.*
*Then from 35,000 throats and more there rose a lusty yell;*
*it rumbled in the Fens, it rattled o'er the Charles;*
*it knocked upon the Back Bay towers and swept o'er the Common flats;*
*for Billy, might Billy, was advancing to the bat.*
*There was ease in Billy's manner as he stepped into his place;*
*there was reserve in Billy's bearing and a calm upon Billy's face.*
*And when, responding to the cheers, he lightly grabbed his bat,*
*no stranger in the crowd could doubt 'twas Billy at the bat.*

*Ten million eyes were on him as he rubbed his hands with dirt;*
*five million hands applauded when he wiped them on his shirt.*
*Then while the writhing closer ground the ball into his hip,*
*patience gleamed in Billy's eyes, a silence upon his lip.*
*And now the leather-covered sphere came hurtling through the air,*
*and Billy stood a-watching it in humble silence there.*
*Close by the sturdy batsman the ball unheeded sped—*
*"I'll take a pitch," said Billy. "Ball one," the umpire said.*
*From bleachers, full of people, there went up a muffled roar,*
*like the beating of the storm-waves on the Cape and Islands' shore.*
*With a smile of Christian charity, the great Billy's visage shone;*
*he stilled the rising tumult; he bade the game go on.*
*He signaled to Rivera, and once more the spheroid spun;*
*but Billy squared to bunt, and the umpire said, "Strike one."*
*"———!" cried the maddened thousands, and echo answered call;*
*but one quick look from Billy and the audience was stalled.*
*They saw his face grow still and quiet, they saw his lack of strain,*
*and they knew that Billy wouldn't let that ball go by again.*
*The fear is gone from Billy's face, his swing will not be late,*
*he taps with easy patience his bat upon the plate.*
*And now the closer holds the ball, and now he lets it go,*
*and now the air is shattered with the force of Billy's blow.*
*Oh, somewhere in this favored land the day has turned to night;*
*the ballparks have gone dark with gloom, and mourn a losing plight;*
*and somewhere fans are crying, and somewhere all is shit;*
*but there is still joy in Boston—mighty Billy got a hit.*

And what did mighty Billy do after he got his mighty hit? He stood on first base and patiently removed one batting glove at a time, and neatly folded them together before handing them back to first base coach Lynn Jones. Meanwhile, Fenway, Boston, New England, and millions more across the country and around the world went absolutely unconscious with joy. But then, mighty Billy was never one to call attention to himself, and thankfully for all Sox fans, because of his trying to be perfect every night, he will never have to.

Because from now on, we fans, as old baseball storytellers, will take that responsibility for him. When we tell our bedtime stories of Red Sox greatness and Red Sox greats, Billy Mueller will surely be one of our favorite characters, and mighty Billy's hit one of our favorite parts of the story.

He will have no dialogue, of course, except perhaps for one single, perfect quote. It comes near the end of the story, after Game Three of the World Series in which Mueller recorded two big hits. It follows a question about how important it was to him to have such a big moment there, in his hometown of St. Louis, in front of his friends and family, in the World Series. By way of response, Bill Mueller, who speaks in clichés and whose words so rarely express anything but humility and deference, summed up for all time how we will remember him in our stories; all in two short, simple sentences.

"I'm not here to analyze it," he said. "I'm here to play."

Perfect.

**idiot RULE:** *Quality is never cliché.*

# Down and Out with Mark Bellhorn

**Mark Bellhorn** shuffles from the on-deck circle to home plate one slow, deliberate step after another, helmet angled down and bat at his side; around him a packed Fenway Park lets out a nervous, hopeful applause. His face is blanched and clammy—with his dark brown, slightly greasy hair curling from beneath his helmet, sideburns inches below his ears and haphazardly blending, at a point, into the two-day growth covering his chin and jaw. A small lump in his right cheek pushes out just below his lower lip, keeping his lips slightly parted at all times. He turns his droopy, tired eyes from umpire to pitcher with a sedate, detached expression—looking as if only moments ago, and without warning, he was nudged from a dead stupor by a teammate on the bench and informed, as he staggered and groped and was handed a bat and helmet, that his presence was required in the batter's box.

## First Impressions

It is the same expression Mark Bellhorn displayed for Sox fans on the first day of spring training, the same expression he held throughout the entire tumultuous regular season, and it is the same expression he holds on a blustery Saturday night in mid-autumn (October 16, 2004) as he comes up in the bottom of the first to face the Yankees' Kevin Brown in Game Three of the ALCS. With the Yankees leading 2-0 in the series and, after only a half inning, 3-0 in the game, both the Sox and Bellhorn are in the process of fighting through painful and untimely slumps—both of which have put their respective seasons in peril, both of which are about to become much, much worse than either could have ever imagined.

Bellhorn presses his helmet against his head and sets his stance, his red socks pulled knee-high against the white of his home uniform. Feet shoulder-width apart and square to the pitcher, he stands almost flat-footed, leaning forward imperceptibly on his toes, knees slightly bent, and windmills the bat around (clockwise) one rotation with both hands and then, letting go with his left hand, one more full rotation with only the right hand before bringing the bat set chest high in front, fingers balancing it lightly and softly strumming the handle.

Brown delivers the first pitch and Bellhorn studies it into Jorge Posada's mitt (*hey look, a baseball*) for ball one. Resetting his stance he steps back in and this time swings late and misses, then follows a third as it passes (*hey look, there's another one*) and claps into Posada's mitt for strike two, sending the Fenway crowd shifting in its seat, sensing a prolonged at-bat of similar observations and similar late, clipping just-foul swings. The fourth pitch, however, is the last of the at-bat as Bellhorn takes a full swing, diving forward, head down on the ball. He turns on his back foot and throws the bat through the strike zone and into his follow-through as his right hand lifts the bat up and out, pointing skyward; and both swing and at-bat end with a second, more unfortunately familiar image as Bellhorn glances back and finds the ball in Posada's mitt. Strike three. Helmet angled down and bat at his side, Bellhorn shuffles away from home plate with one slow, deliberate step after another as Fenway shifts and grumbles around him.

# Down Swinging

Mark Bellhorn has struck out. Again. And although this has only been his first at-bat of the night, both he and the Fenway crowd now grumbling uncomfortably have grown far too familiar with this sequence, its patterns, and this final image—the bat held high, Bellhorn glancing back to the ball—having been given so many opportunities over the course of Bellhorn's first season with the Red Sox to examine it in detail.

Over the course of a Red Sox season marked by irregularity and inconsistency, by shifting lineups and unpredictable weather, the image of Mark Bellhorn striking out has remained one of the few reliable constants in the life of the Sox and their fans. From a casual, barely noticed spring training strikeout under the Florida sun, to a gray and meager swing and miss on a damp and drizzly October evening at Fenway, the Bellhorn strikeout has been a steady beat throughout an unsteady season.

Prior to his strikeout in Game Three, he has struck out twice in the ALDS, four times in the ALCS, and a team-leading, league-leading 177 times in the regular season, more than any other switch hitter in the history of the game, and more than anyone else in the majors in 2004 except for Cincinnati's Adam Dunn, who set the MLB record for a single season with his astounding 195.

He has, over the course of the season, struck out in every inning, on every day of the week, and in every month. He has struck out on crisp, cool April evenings when the season was young and the stat sheet thin with single-digits, and he has struck out on thick, muggy-hot August afternoons before sweaty crowds, the late-season, late-summer stat sheet fat and full. He has struck out at Fenway, wearing his home whites, and wearing his Sunday reds, and he has struck out wearing his road gray in ballparks and stadiums from Maryland to California, from Florida to Washington. He has struck out during languid, quiet games in Toronto, the Sox leading big and the game a series of set-pieces the players lazily follow, and he has struck out with runners on in the tense late-innings of crucial, epic grudge matches against the Yankees. He has struck out against right-handed pitchers and lefties, against veteran All-Stars and fresh-faced teenagers making their Major League debuts, on fastballs up and change-ups down, on breaking balls off the plate and (far more frequently) on sliders down and in, on 0-2 pitches and (far more frequently) on 3-2 counts, with two outs and with none out, to lead off an inning or to make the last out of an inning or the last out of a game, on lush grass lawns and rubbery artificial turf, indoors and outdoors, in the rain and in the sun, in the cold and in the heat, in the day and in the night. He even struck out on his birthday (twice).

And yet somehow Mark Bellhorn shuffles from the on-deck circle to home plate to lead off the fourth inning, not a trace of the 184 strikeouts he has endured over the course of the season and playoffs to be found behind his tired eyes as he steps in to face Javier Vasquez for his third at-bat of the night. In the third, he had battled back from an 0-2 count to draw a walk from the struggling Brown, but since then the game has gone horribly wrong for both Bellhorn and his teammates, the Yankees now leading 11-6 in only the fourth inning of an already exhausting battle of attrition. Bellhorn watches Vasquez's first pitch snap by for a strike, swings at and misses his second and, settling a bit, watches the third go by for a ball. He looks out now, holds the bat lightly at his chest, rolls the chaw in his lower lip, and waits for the 1-2. Vasquez throws a slider down and in and Bellhorn swings, his head down and the end of his bat lofted high in the air, pointing straight up to the night sky. He pauses, then peeks back. Strike three. Mark Bellhorn has struck out, again (185), and the Fenway crowd rumbles and groans as shouts and curses now ring out from the bleachers.

## MONSTER minutiae

Bellhorn's already unsightly numbers look even worse, if possible, when one considers the fact that Adam Dunn played in 23 more games and stepped to the plate 45 more times than Bellhorn. If Bellhorn had played the same number of games at his steady rate of around 1⅓ strikeouts per game, he would have likely shattered the record with a jaw-dropping 206 strikeouts.

## Stepping Up

It was never supposed to be like this, of course, not for Bellhorn and certainly not for the Sox. When the Red Sox acquired Bellhorn in December of 2003 from the Colorado Rockies (for a player to be named later), it was with the intention of adding depth to their already stellar infield, providing a solid backup for the Gold Glove–winning Pokey Reese, whom they would sign later in the month to start at second, ahead of Bellhorn. It was never meant to be then, if for no other reason than because Bellhorn was never meant to step to the plate enough times to even consider striking out so often. But then something unintended happened: Nomar Garciaparra suffered a bruised Achilles in spring training, a minor injury that would keep him out of the Opening Day lineup and would, at the same time, insert Bellhorn in the lineup next to Reese in the middle infield.

Bellhorn took his position at second on Opening Day, as he would day after day through April, into May, and on into June, by which time he had compiled a considerable number of strikeouts but also, and more significantly, a considerable number of walks. Mixed in with a handful of hits, Bellhorn had shown an ability to do what was most valued by his manager and front office—he got on base. Still, the strikeouts stood out, both in the newspapers and in the minds of most Sox fans, who by this time had begun a daily vigil over the return of their starting shortstop, anticipating the expected return of their projected lineup and the projected return of Mark Bellhorn to the bench. (*Yeah, he's okay, for now. He'll do, I guess.*) As Nomar's return approached the discussion which had simmered in casual conversation all season finally came to a boil, and Sox fans everywhere took sides and made their cases in the Pokey v. Bellhorn debate. The campaign was never Bellhorn's to win.

## What's-His-Name at Second

Part of this had to do with style, which the silky Reese exudes both on the field and on camera and which Bellhorn, clammy-faced and silent, does not. On the field he does little to invite attention to himself, says even less, and in the boisterous carnival that is the Boston clubhouse—with more flamboyant spectacles of sight and sound on display outside the lockers of Pedro Martinez and Kevin Millar and

Johnny Damon, among others—the shy, quiet second baseman was most often passed by and passed over, a distinctly uncharismatic figure on this distinctly charismatic team. Early on in the season he was given the standard get-to-know-the-new-Sox treatment—a feature article in the Globe, a feature piece on the NESN pregame show—but once these passed the microphones and cameras were quick to move on to see what Manny was up to now, and to hear what Schilling had to say next. And so Bellhorn slipped away, from the media and from the fans, seated on the bench with his lips slightly parted, two-days' growth across his jaw and a weary look on his face, he watched Reese step to the plate as Fenway echoed with its newfound chant, warm and giving—*Po-Kee, Po-Kee, Po-Kee.* And yet his name continued to show up on Terry Francona's lineup card, game after game, week after week, and he continued to come to bat, continued to take pitches, continued to draw walks, continued to strike out, continued to play; and when Nomar returned in early June, Bellhorn stayed in the lineup, and was given only a few games off in which Reese started at second. Then, ten days after Nomar's return, Reese tore a ligament in his thumb and Bellhorn was once again back in the lineup at second—where he continued to come up to bat, continued to walk, continued to strike out.

## Down Looking

So by the time Bellhorn shuffles to the plate with one on and one out in the sixth of Game Three of the ALCS, with the Sox now in the nauseous stages of a bitter 13-6 freefall, his mere presence is viewed by many Sox fans as simply another unintended and unfortunate element in this season in which nothing, it seems, has gone the way it was supposed to. With Vasquez still on the mound and Orlando Cabrera taking a lead off second behind him, Bellhorn swings and clips the first pitch of the at-bat foul for strike one, then swings and misses for strike two as a low, sinking moan ripples throughout Fenway. (*Bellhahn, you're killin' me, kid!*) He watches a third miss for ball one—running the count, once again, to 1-2—then steps back, looks over the bat, and steps in to take his stance.

Vasquez delivers a slider down and Bellhorn throws the bat out after it, head down, raising the end up high above on the follow-through. He peeks back, and Fenway winces with him. Mark Bellhorn has struck out, again (186), and the Sox are losing to the Yankees, again, and the series and the season and the summer are all slipping away, again; and the heartache and the loss and the dull, suffocating humiliation of having been duped into believing that this game and this series and this season could be any different from every other has begun to seep through the sweaters and jackets and fleeces around Fenway, again. And the deep, echoing boos and sharp, distant curses that cascade down over him fall not on his shoulders alone, and bemoan not only his failure, and mourn not only the loss of the game and the (inevitable) loss of the series and season, but likewise express how painfully Fenway recognizes itself in the fate of our second baseman, shuffling off the field, and how very deeply the sadness and embarrassment of this realization is felt among Red Sox fans everywhere.

Failure in life is an inevitability, but perhaps more so in baseball than in most other areas—part of daily life in a sport where the team that won more games than any other in the league (St. Louis) still lost fifty-seven times over the course of the summer, and in which the player who hit safely more often than any other player in the history of the game (Ichiro) still made an out and thus failed 442 times during one season.

But there are different ways of failing, some more dignified than others. In baseball the dignified out is the sharp line drive snared by a fortuitously placed infielder, the long drive run down on the warning track by a ranging outfielder, the tough 12-pitch at bat which ends in a grounder to the right side and pushes a runner to second, thus sacrificing one's self for the benefit of the team. All are among the more respectable ways for a hitter to fail, each allowing the retired man to jog back to the dugout with his head held high, perhaps even to receive a few encouraging slaps from his teammates in acknowledgment of his efforts.

Then, of course, there are somewhat less noble ways of failing, and in baseball none is less noble, none is less respectable or less dignified than the clean and simple strikeout. It is, for a hitter, a base and utter failure to achieve anything close to his goal of hitting the ball solidly afield—a complete, thorough failure. The hitter who has recently struck out returns to the dugout silently, avoided by the next man up and skirted (lest the pallor of failure somehow rub off) by the man stepping from the dugout to the on-deck circle. He steps down into the dugout without a word as his teammates stare out onto the field; he quietly removes his helmet and settles it back in its place, slides his bat back in its slot and walks down through the dugout (*click, click, click*) to quietly take his seat on the bench, alone.

Failure such as this is quickly dismissed, forgotten, and moved past until the next turn in the lineup comes about and the count is reset, 0-0, for the hitter to try again. When this type of failure is repeated often enough over a long enough timeline (say 186 times over 144 games), it can become much more difficult to forget, and weigh much heavier on a conscience as general disappointment and regret are pushed, little by little, strikeout by strikeout, toward something darker and more troubling—nearing something much closer to embarrassment.

Similarly, there are ways in which a team and an organization can fail with dignity, and there are ways in which they can fail without dignity, or grace, or respect. Of the former, we think of the undermanned team that fights the good fight, that battles against great odds and makes the game a game and competes down to the very last out, in the end succumbing to an overwhelming disadvantage in resources and talent and experience. Of the latter, we have most recently (as recently as October 16, 2004) thought of the Red Sox. To repeatedly come ever closer to the edge of success and yet repeatedly fall to evermore unlikely and unfortunate twists of fate and failure—to lose pennants on soft pop flies, to lose championships on a medley of errors both mental and physical, to lose seasons to highly questionable managerial decisions—these graceless individual failures may be managed individually, but over time they tend to build one upon the other, until over enough time (say, 86 years) they become very difficult to step away from, even more difficult to forget, and all but impossible to remove. And at a certain point, their collective strain begins to weigh much more heavily than the sum of each individual year, and as the whole of these solitary failures begin to darken as they too, like a season of strikeouts, begin to harden into something much darker, much more troubling—into something much closer to humiliation.

It is a terrible, nauseating moment then when Fenway as a whole looks down at Mark Bellhorn and watches him strike out for the third time and fall to his lowest point of the season, just as Sox fans everywhere hit the exact same low at exactly the same moment. The night, at that moment, turns from upsetting to embarrassing as the weight of 186 strikeouts and 86 years finally tip an unseen balance over in the hearts and minds of Red Sox fans. And by the time Bellhorn comes up again in the eighth for his final at-bat and quickly falls behind two strikes, the jeers and curses have thinned to a few head-shaking sighs from the handful of shell-shocked fans who have stayed long enough to see it. Two pitches later, on a 1-2 count, when Mark Bellhorn takes a fastball on the outside corner for a called third strike and strikes out for the fourth time in one night and the 187th time in one season, no groans or curses rain down from the empty red seats surrounding him and he shuffles back to the dugout—one slow, deliberate step at a time—in near silence.

## Stepping Up, Once Again

Mark Bellhorn shuffles from the on-deck circle to home plate one slow, deliberate step after another, helmet angled down and bat at his side; and around him a packed Fenway Park lets out a nervous, hopeful applause. His face blanched and clammy—with his dark brown, slightly greasy hair curling from beneath his helmet, sideburns inches below his ears and haphazardly blending, at a point, into the two-day growth covering his chin and jaw. A small lump in his right cheek pushes out just below his lower lip, keeping his lips slightly parted at all times. He turns his droopy, tired eyes from umpire to pitcher with a sedate, detached expression. It is the same expression Mark Bellhorn displayed for Sox fans on the first day of spring training, the same expression he held throughout the entire tumultuous regular season, the same expression he held exactly one week earlier when he struck out four times in Game Three of the ALCS, the same expression he holds now, on this crisp, windy Saturday night in mid-autumn (October 23, 2004) as he comes up in the bottom of the eighth to face Cardinals reliever Julian Tavares in Game One of the World Series.

The game—a tumultuous roller coaster spiked with drastic swings of momentum and filled with bizarre, head-shaking play on both sides—is tied, 9-9, with Jason Varitek standing on first and one out, and with both teams having blown through reams of opportunities to take control of the game. It has by this point become a much more desperate, tooth-and-nail struggle than the opening game of a seven-game set would suggest.

Bellhorn steps to the plate having already singled once and walked twice. He has not struck out. Red socks pulled knee-high to his white home uniform, he presses his helmet and sets his stance. Feet shoulder-width apart and square to the pitcher, he stands almost flat-footed, leaning forward imperceptibly on his toes, knees slightly bent, and windmills the bat around (clockwise) one rotation with both hands and then, letting go with his left hand, one more full rotation with only the right hand before bringing the bat set chest high in front, fingers balancing it lightly and softly strumming the handle.

The first pitch is a fastball inside and Bellhorn jackknifes away as the ball cuts in over the inside corner for strike one. Resetting now he looks back out, waits, and on the second pitch takes a low hook-swing at an inside slider, pulling it high down the right field line before it drifts left to right (the flag above center pointing its way) back into the grandstands, well foul and well short of the yellow Pesky Pole. Bellhorn steps back to the plate, resets his stance, and this time takes a breaking ball off the plate for ball one. The count, once again, is 1-2. The next pitch from Tavares is the same pitch that Mark Bellhorn has struck out on repeatedly all season long—a slider, down and in, under his hands—and as Bellhorn dives in and swings through it, head down, he follows through with the end of the bat held high in the air, pointing straight up into the night sky.

This time, though, he looks up. The ball sails high out over the right field line, drifting back and hooking slightly to the right as every Sox player jumps to the top step of the dugout and every Sox fan jumps to his feet and we all for a moment lean our collective bodies forward and wave our collective hands and hold our collective breaths as the ball sails down into the lights and strikes the top, inside grate of the yellow Pesky Pole. All of Fenway erupts in instant, delirious celebration as the ball lands softly to the green outfield grass below. And somewhere through the high-fives and hugs and frantic, hurried calls to friends across the country, beneath the shower of shouts and cheers of joy, Mark Bellhorn circles the bases, a quick skip on one heel before he steps on home plate and high-fives Johnny Damon and falls into the mobbing arms of his teammates waiting on the top step.

## *Atta'boy Bellhahn*

Four nights later, in St. Louis, when the Red Sox won Game Four of the World Series and Mark Bellhorn rushed out of the dugout with his teammates to celebrate the team's first World Championship in 86 years, there might have been those who saw this moment as a heroic achievement for Red Sox fans everywhere. As the champagne corks popped and the gold trophy was presented, there may have been those who saw in this long-awaited celebration the virtue of persistence by both a team and a people; and this, to a degree, is understandable.

But somehow this misses, if only slightly, the true mark of character that Red Sox fans have throughout the years borne by example, because it was not within the mad dash four-game sweep to a championship that the true character of the Red Sox experience was revealed. (This familiar, annual celebration is carried out by more casual teams to the joy of more casual fans.) Instead, it was found ten days prior on a chilly Sunday night in Boston, when 35,000 packed Fenway and millions across the country settled in front of their televisions and radios to watch and listen to the Sox, no matter how bad it got, no matter how dark it looked, no matter how painful the outcome. The fans who returned to Fenway for Game Four with the Sox down 0-3, embarrassed and all but technically eliminated, were the same fans who had returned in 1979 after 1978 broke their hearts; they were the same fans who returned in 1987 after 1986 nearly broke their spirits; and they were the same fans who returned to Opening Day, 2004, after the 2003 season once again fell gracelessly to failure.

If there is any virtue in persistence, then it was not to be found in the crowded streets and packed bars and lively homes where Sox fans celebrated our championship, but in the quiet living rooms and dour bars and in the nervous, stubborn faces in the crowd at Fenway on October 17, 2004, as Sox fans returned to our team one day after the most bitter, most humiliating of failures. Because while there are many ways to strike out (both in life and baseball), there is only one true way to do so heroically (in either), and that is by stepping back up to the plate.

As for Mark Bellhorn, shuffling off the field and into the mob of teammates waiting for him on the top step of the dugout, it seems once again Sox fans can look down upon him and recognize a reflection of ourselves. Having fallen again and again, having been given up on over and over, Bellhorn now sits in the dugout with a strange expression on his face, one many Sox fans see on replay for the first time all season. It is Mark Bellhorn's smile. Sitting on the bench and surrounded by teammates he grins wide and full, the lump at the lower left of his face sliding down as he does, and makes a hooking motion with his flat left hand—mimicking the flight of the ball before it struck the pole. As he sits there among the congratulations of his peers and the shower of wild celebration still echoing down around him from his fans, there may be those who would call Mark Bellhorn a hero.

We may agree with the label, but the timing of its honor seems more than a bit belated. Because while his dramatic home run speaks a great deal about Mark Bellhorn's ability as a hitter, the true mark of his character came much earlier, on that same chilly and nervous Sunday night when he stepped up to the plate in the bottom of the second, having struck out four times the night before and 187 times overall. True, Mark Bellhorn was the hero of Game One of the World

Series, but his most heroic moments in 2004 were not the thunder and lightning of his home run, but instead the much quieter, much more lonely trials on the bench after each embarrassing strikeout. Whatever heroism we grant him deserves to be given not for the one quick, dramatic swing that launched his historic home run, but instead upon the 187 triumphs of individual perseverance when he picked himself up off the bench after striking out, shuffled out from the on-deck circle, and stepped back up to the plate.

**idiot RULE:** *It's not how you go down, it's whether or not you step back up.*

# Chapter  8

# Deep Depth

## How to Play Shortstop for the Boston Red Sox

**It goes like this:** With your right hand, knock fists top, bottom, top, then together; then pat the right shoulder one, two, three; throw the right hand up and back; then to the chin *and forget about it.* That's what you do when you see Manny in the dugout right after he hits a home run. If it's Ortiz, it goes more like this: knock top, bottom, top; three shoulder taps; back; then both arms up, big up for Big Papi. But if it's Millar, you mix the whole thing up, and do this: high five top, bottom, back of the hand (2x); down (2x); then slap hands back, forward, back, forward; then draw your imaginary six-shooters and fire it up, cowboy style. (Don't worry; he thinks it looks cool.)

Say it's Tek, though. Say he rips a shot in Anaheim to tie the game and everybody's all pumped and hugging and giving high-fives. Just stand in line and wait your turn and when you see Tek stick his big fist out, hold yours up and give it a knock, a nod, maybe a quick, *that'a boy Tek* (just remember, do not hug the catcher).

And if it's Petey, coming down the steps after the sixth, knowing he's done and knowing he just pitched the biggest game of his life in the World Series, and acting all cool like he knew it all along, just give the man a hug. That's enough.

Then in the ninth, as Foulke is punching through those last three, make sure you find your boy Reese, give him a nod with two outs left. And when the ump rings up that final out, run out and meet Pokey on the infield grass and go: fist top, bottom, top; three pats to the shoulders; and then jump as high as you can in the air with your arms out and your head up and a big grin on your face, like you just won the World Series or something.

## 1. Pick Up Your Uniform

You won't know all this stuff at first, not on that first day, when you show up in the clubhouse and all the reporters (more than you saw in

Montreal in a week) crush around you like you're some bigshot, like all of a sudden you're Barry Bonds or something. Relax, unpack your stuff and look into the camera and tell everybody you're *just here to help the team win*, that you're just here to play. Eventually they'll go away, and you can catch your breath. A guy you don't know will ask you what number you want and when you say 44, because that's what your pops wore, he'll say it's already taken, so you'll take 36. (Don't worry, later on one of the other new guys, Roberts, will give it to you; make sure you thank him when he does.)

Be sure to let the equipment manager know you want your pants and jersey big and baggy. You want your pants down to your cleats and your jersey nice and roomy—nothing too tight. You can keep your thin moustache and the little patch you've been growing on your chin, but you'll probably want to let out the braids you had with the Expos, trim it down to a nice little 'fro.

## 2. Try to Relax

Your first game in Minnesota is probably going to be strange, but just try to go up there and get a good swing. If you see a fastball, hit it out of the ballpark. That'll help you relax some. After that, try to hit everything hard on a line. The pitchers over here already know you're a fastball hitter, so you're going to see nothing but breaking stuff for about three weeks. You're going to hit a ton of balls into the dirt. You're going to pop up on bad pitches and get all pissed at yourself and slam your bat. Don't worry.

When the reporters ask if you're trying too hard tell them the truth, tell them you're just trying to hit the ball. (Some of them will understand this, others won't; but you can't help it either way, so don't worry about it.)

When you come home to Boston, try not to be overwhelmed by Fenway. You'll see more fans packed in there than you saw in a month with the Expos, and every one of them will react to every single move you make, every pitch in every at-bat. They'll be patient with you when you first get there, for awhile. But keep popping up, keep hitting balls into the dirt, and eventually you'll start to hear it from them—a faint grumble at first, not a real boo but something there, enough, and you will be able to hear it.

## RED SOX NATION

On July 31, 2004, the Red Sox traded Nomar Garciaparra. In return for Garciaparra, the Sox received shortstop Orlando Cabrera from the Montreal Expos and first baseman Doug Mientkiewicz from the Minnesota Twins. The move, which sent one of the most beloved figures in Red Sox history to the Chicago Cubs, was a polarizing moment for many Sox fans, and was viewed at the time as the biggest gamble of general manager Theo Epstein's career. The merits and effects of the deal were debated throughout the season and after, but the immediate impact on the team and its fans was that on that day, for the first time in nearly a decade, the Boston Red Sox had a new shortstop.

That's when you've got to rely on your glove. Don't carry what happened at the plate out onto the field with you; just take your position, stay on your toes, and react. That will get you through. People will tell you that you're only here for your defense anyway, that's all they want, so just relax and keep your glove down.

One night, though, when things are starting to go really, really bad for you at the plate, you'll make an error. Nothing big, you'll just let down your guard a bit, try to start the throw before the ball's in your glove and *bang*, E6. Expect Fenway to boo. Then, with this play still in the back of your mind, you'll make another, in the same game, E6, and then you'll really hear it, like you've never heard it before. And just when you think that's the worst of it, you'll get an easy one right at you, and you'll field and throw no problem, an easy play. But you'll hear it again, only this time mock cheers, cheering you like they're surprised you even made *that* play. You'll feel horrible. You'll feel sick. When you get to the locker room, dress without a word, and when the reporters all crush around you tell them, *not tonight fellas*, and get out. Go home.

## 3. When You Get Your Pitch, Hit It

The next day, take your cuts in the cage like you always do, take your grounders at short, relax a bit, joke around with Manny some. When your name is announced and you hear the boos, don't even flinch—don't even act like you heard a thing. Just run out onto the field and pat your glove and play catch with Millar.

Later on in the game, when you come up in the ninth with the game tied and Damon on first, take your stance in the box like you always do—spread your feet wide and give yourself a nice good base, get back on that back leg and keep your hands up above that shoulder, farther back, get a good lean and make sure your chin touches your left shoulder—stay back. Forget about the numbers out on the scoreboard. Forget about the errors the night before. Forget about all the reporters and all the questions and all the shouts from the crowd, and just stay back on that breaking ball.

When you get it—when you see that little red dot that tells you the slider's coming—keep your head down on it and bring your hands right to it—there—and follow through as you feel that nice jolt when the ball jumps off your bat. Now run. Sprint around first and watch the ball kick off the wall and hang above center, a sure double. Dig to second and give a quick peek back as Johnny sprints home, slides in safe, and the whole place goes crazy and makes a sound like you've never heard in your life. Ever.

Then jog out to where your teammates pile around Damon at the plate, and cover your head when all of a sudden the whole team surrounds you and yells and slaps you on the head and jumps up and down. When you stagger out of the pile, smiling wide, take a look around—look at how happy all the people are, look at how happy you've made them.

In the clubhouse, don't even bother to try to undress. You won't have the room or the time to even start. Just stand at your locker and answer each question one at a time. Say something nice about the fans. Mention your teammates. Tell everyone you're just glad to help the team get a win, and try not to smile too wide when you say it.

## 4. Just Play

After that, you're golden. Get to the ballpark early every day, sign a few autographs outside the player's parking lot, and wave to the fans around the batting cage. When you have a moment in the dugout or in the clubhouse, learn Manny's dance. Then learn Papi's. Have some fun. Don't be intimidated by Yankee Stadium when you go there (it's grass and dirt, just like all the others). Step up to the plate and get yourself a big hit there too, a single through the right side to bring in the winning run. When you get to first, don't forget to point up to the sky and let your pops up in heaven know that one was for him.

Make the plays you need to make at short. Don't press. Just field and throw, *bang-bang*, just like you've always done. Same ground balls here as in Montreal, same distance from short to first as back in Colombia.

And don't be afraid to be the hero again, either. When you come up in extra innings against Baltimore, and your team needs a win and not much is happening, get a pitch that looks good and go ahead and take a big home run swing. Rip one up over the wall in left and then sprint around the bases, flip off your helmet coming down the third base line, and with the whole place roaring and your whole team gathered around home, give one big skip and jump on up into that crowd. Go on and be the hero.

## 5. Celebrate

When the postseason comes, you'll be fine. You'll know all your teammates, you'll know all the dance moves, and you'll know all the reporters. Do a few interviews. Have your picture taken a few times. Sign some more autographs. You'll be comfortable in Fenway by that point, no worries there. And when the games start out in Anaheim, don't even think anything of it, just go play baseball. Make your plays at short and give yourself a chance at the plate; don't give in on those breaking balls, make them throw you a fastball every once in awhile.

You won't believe how much hype will surround some of those games; you'll see more reporters, and more cameras, and more microphones, than you've ever seen in your whole career. Everywhere you go, on the street, in the news, in the paper, no one will talk about anything else; everyone will be talking about The Series. They'll cover the ballpark in red, white, and blue. They'll bring in some bigshots to sing the anthem and they'll have all sorts of ceremonies and awards and presentations.

But then eventually, you'll run out onto the field and the pitcher will get the ball, and the ump will point out and the game will start. Just play. Play the game the way you played it to get here, to get to the United States, to get to Boston, to get to The Series. Play hard and play without fear.

When someone hits a home run and comes back into the dugout, give him a hug and do the dance he taught you. Smile, have a good time, play. When you've played every game, and you've taken every at-bat, you may find yourself standing out at shortstop in Busch Stadium in Game Four—right behind Foulkie and looking in at your boy Edgar (you and he, two shortstops from Colombia, together here in the big time) at the plate. Go ahead and take your stance just like normal, stay on your toes and hold your glove out. When the ball clips back to Foulke and he takes a few steps and flips to Mientkiewicz at first, just run in and throw your glove and jump as high as you can in the air, and celebrate like you just won the World Series.

**idiot RULE:** *Read the manual.*

# Mientkiewiczetcetera

**History always remembers the man** with the ball in his glove at the end. No matter the role of the player, no matter the circumstances of the play, if you find yourself holding the baseball the moment your team wins the World Series, you can be sure you will live in memory as long as fans have memories at all. And your ecstatic, joyous first leap into the air will outlive even those memories, passed down by generations of television producers (from video, to digital, to whatever may come next) as the single-clip evidence of a championship.

## Changlng Dugouts

Catchers and first basemen must know this, as they take their stances in the last inning of a deciding World Series game. They may realize, *this could be it*; but more than likely they do not, not at the moment anyway (too busy thinking about outs and such). And so, more than likely, Doug Mientkiewicz does not quite realize when he takes his stance behind first, punches his glove, and crouches down low as Renteria looks out and Foulke looks in, that the next five seconds of his life will be committed to baseball eternity. A moment later, when he clasps the ball in his black firstbaseman's glove and leaps high into the air, feet together and finger pointing (no. 1), nothing is left but to feel joy, nothing is left to realize but that the Red Sox are World Champions.

But history knows. History recognizes this image of the first baseman leaping high as the precise moment of achievement, and fixes it there—upon hundreds of video reels and on thousands of rolls of film and within millions of individual memories. *Click-click.* That is it. That is the moment the Red Sox won the World Series, and the man with the ball in his glove there is Doug Mientkiewicz. *Come again?* That's Mientkiewicz, M-i-e-n-t-k—surely we have learned by now. Still, we imagine history having a hard time with the name, just as Sox fans did when it first appeared on a Red Sox scorecard during a tumultuous trip to Minnesota in late July. One half of perhaps the biggest trade in club history, Mientkiewicz's own personal drama slipped somewhat into the background behind the trade's more incendiary, more immediate fallout in Boston.

## *MONSTER* minutiae

Mientkiewicz's somewhat unwieldy last name was the story the media picked up on first, and rounds of half-joking questions came about the spelling and nicknames. Mientkiewicz bore them all admirably with patience and in good humor, despite the fact that he must by now have heard these same questions and jokes, millions of times at every stop in his career. A good sport, this one.

Meanwhile, the timing of the trade sent Mientkiewicz on one of the most difficult and awkward walks in all of sports. He gathered up his belongings from his Twins locker—from the only professional organization he had ever known—said his goodbyes to a group of teammates he had grown up playing alongside, and walked through the Metrodome corridors to the visiting clubhouse, where he unpacked his belongings and pulled on a gray Red Sox road jersey. For this walk alone, he earned the respect of the fans (in both cities). The Red Sox moved on, and so did Mientkiewicz, and over the final two months of the season he became a familiar face behind first base (and once, memorably, at second), primarily near the end of Red Sox wins.

## Difficult Name, Easy Fit

A dusty, unkempt breed of player, Mientkiewicz looked the part of an old Sox gamer with his red stockings pulled knee-high, red sleeves roughly cut off just below his jersey sleeves and flapping around his arms, blue elbow brace on his left arm, and scruffy goatee on his chin. With pine tar on his helmet, a black shin guard on his right ankle, and bare hands in the batter's box, he brings a distinctly Nixonian presence to the dugout, and for this Fenway took to him almost immediately.

And took to his presence around first, too, as Mientkiewicz quickly and consistently showed his worth picking difficult infield throws out of the dirt with a smooth, confident sweep of the glove—a natural fielder, a fielder to trust. And so when the postseason began and the Sox grabbed early leads, and took those leads into the later innings, fans began to instinctively look down the dugout for No. 13 to grab his black firstbaseman's glove; wanting him on that base in the end. And in the end, in every single postseason game the Red Sox won, right down to the very end, he was.

Although a talented, well-rounded player deserving of a spot in any lineup, Mientkiewicz was brought to Boston to play a specific role, to fill a specific need, and to his credit (although at times it surely must have been difficult), he did. He could not have known when he took this role that history would single him out—it is neither why you play the game nor why you work for a championship, but then sometimes it happens nonetheless. You end up out there in Game Four of the World Series, in the bottom of the ninth with two outs, crouching into position behind first base, waiting, and then the ball is chopped back to the mound, and you slide into position and hold your glove out and (already smiling now) wait for the soft lob and then catch it, just like you were brought here to do—and that's it. You leap high in the air, as high as you can, and suddenly the world goes bleary with joy.

And then, years later, when you and we are less inclined to leaping in the air, there will come a moment when we are watching a baseball game on television, the first game of some lazy, midsummer doubleheader, and the announcer will make a passing reference. Perhaps it's an anniversary (2024, 2029), perhaps some team is facing a great deficit in the standings, perhaps it is simply the Sox who are on and there is a sudden need for a pleasant reminder—and a producer somewhere will say, *roll the clip*, and the announcer will say, *let's have a look back*, and suddenly there you will be, on all of our screens again just as you were so many years ago, young and agile and suddenly joyous as you leap high into the air.

**idiot RULE:** *If you only have one job, make sure you do it well.*

# Doug's Turn

**Backup catchers,** like backup quarterbacks, need patience. They need to be willing and able to catch (obviously), to call a game, to have a strong arm to second, to be effective at the plate, and at the very least be competent on the base paths. But as much as any of these qualities, the backup catcher needs to be able to do nothing—to be able to wait, and be patient. He needs to be able to occupy himself in the bullpen for long stretches of the season, catching a reliever who is about to enter the game or simply hanging over the bullpen wall working a mouthful of seeds. And at this the Sox backup catcher, Doug Mirabelli, excels.

Throughout the season, we have watched him there in the bullpen, firing seeds at great length and with great accuracy. We have seen him lean back against the wall between innings and stare up at the video board, watching a replay of the previous night's highlights, fascinated. We have watched fans in the bleachers wave to him, and we have watched him wave back. Doug Mirabelli, a man of good humor and indefatigable patience, seems to have all that it takes to be a great backup catcher. None of which should distract us from the fact that Doug Mirabelli also has all that it takes to be a good catcher, period.

## Doug, You're Up

Acquired from Texas in mid-season 2001 after an injury to Jason Varitek, Mirabelli is an inch shorter and ten pounds lighter than the Sox starter (with the weight somehow less compact) and has the full, round face and quick, broad smile of a favorite uncle. On the Sox bench (where he was occasionally fitted for an in-game microphone) and in his conversations with the media, he displays a loose, jocular attitude and a quick, often self-deprecating wit—the kind of guy who knows how to entertain himself and others through the long, eventless yawns that occasionally surface during the 162-game baseball season.

He takes this demeanor with him to the plate, without batting gloves, wristbands, or sleeves. and his forward stance and loose waving of the bat in his bare hands always looks as if the opportunity to bat has been a surprise, as if he were in the back of the clubhouse playing cards at the time and someone has just now called to him, *Doug, hey, Doug, you're up.* He then bounds up from the table and jogs to the dugout, grabs a bat and helmet, and steps up (*Whew, made it*).

Once at the plate, however, Mirabelli shows us that it was not, in fact, his wit or his ability to spit seeds that brought him to the elite level of major league catchers (of which there are around sixty or seventy on the planet). With a quick, sweeping swing from an upright stance, Mirabelli gets to most fastballs he sees. And although he only plays once every five games, and therefore only bats four or five times a week, and although among those four or five at-bats a week, he may only see one bad, hanging breaking ball a week, when he does see it, Mirabelli does not often miss—this season in particular. In the almost sixty games Mirabelli appeared in over the 162-game season, he hit 9 home runs, drove in 34 runs, and hit .281 overall, making his production-to-appearance ratio right up there with some of the best catchers in the league.

We know he can hit; and we know he can catch, as he has exclusively handled the difficult knucklers of Tim Wakefield over the past two seasons. He could, we assume from this, prove himself a reliable and effective starting catcher on some other major league lineup. But this is not what the Red Sox have asked him to do. What they asked him to do is more than just hit, more than just catch, and more than just be patient—they want him to do all three. As a backup catcher, he is asked to mill around the bullpen game after game; lean against the top step of the dugout and spit seeds onto the grass; and then, after all this waiting, be able to step up when called for and perform. What makes Mirabelli valuable to the Red Sox, what made him such an important piece in the picture of their championship, is his ability to do exactly that consistently and effectively.

## Doug, You're Starting

Mirabelli did not play in the ALDS. He had only one at-bat in the ALCS. And yet, after sitting and waiting, after spitting seeds and watching the video board and joking with his teammates in the dugout through the majority of the first ten games of the postseason, Doug Mirabelli was the starting catcher in Game One of the World Series. He had been patient, had waited, and now, when he steps up to the plate in the third inning of the first World Series game at Fenway in almost two decades, catcher Doug Mirabelli rips an 0-2 fastball off Woody Williams high up off the wall for a single, moving Bill Mueller from first to third. He later came around to score on a Cabrera single, and returns to the dugout to high-fives and pats on the back before sitting down to strap on his shin guards.

Backup catchers need to be patient and able to wait their turn, but they also need to be able to perform at the highest level in one of their sport's most demanding positions once that turn comes up. While many are capable of the former, and some are capable of the latter, very few are able to do both. Very few are able to wait and wait and wait, and then instantly perform. It is not an easy job, and although it is perhaps not the role Doug Mirabelli would have chosen for himself, it is the role he was asked to play. Thankfully for the Red Sox and their fans, he was willing and able to. And now, after all these years of being patient, none of us—not Mirabelli, the Sox, or us fans—need to wait any longer.

**idiot RULE:** *When your turn comes, take it.*

$$(dr(x - y) < (n) + (7) + (s) + (r)) = SB$$

**It is a relatively simple equation:** Dave Roberts' rate of speed (dr) must cover the distance between first base and second base (x), minus the lead he takes off first (y), before the pitch delivered by Mariano Rivera covers the distance from the mound to home plate (r), plus the time it takes catcher Jorge Posada to catch and release (s), plus the time it takes his throw to cover the distance between home plate and second base (n), plus the time it takes shortstop Derek Jeter to catch and tag the on-rushing Roberts (7). Simple, really.

If he does not, if: $dr(x - y) > (7) + (n) + (s) + (r)$, the Sox, down a run in the bottom of the ninth of Game Four and down three games in the ALCS, will be two outs away from their season ending in the most devastating way imaginable–swept, at Fenway, by the Yankees—and will likely go down in history as the most disappointing/underachieving team in the long and disappointing history of Red Sox baseball.

But if he does, if: $dr(x - y) < (r) + (s) + (n) + (7)$, then the Sox will have the tying run in scoring position with no outs and Bill Mueller at the plate, and with one base hit the season could be extended one more inning—and who knows what might happen then?

# The Uncommon Variable

Fortunately for the Red Sox and their fans, Dave Roberts has been brought to Boston, in what will forever be remembered as the *other* deadline trade of 2004, to achieve this very task of turning (>) into (<). At the time of the deal that sent a Sox minor leaguer to Los Angeles for Roberts, another trade grabbed most of the headlines in Boston and throughout baseball. The move for Roberts though, the other trade, filled a significant role on the Sox roster which, for most of the season (and, truthfully, throughout most of the organization's history) lacked purpose on the base paths.

Roberts took up No. 31 and for most of the last two months of the season, took up a spot on the Sox bench. He appeared late in a number of games, and started a handful, but other than a few scattered hits and at least one memorable, game-saving catch at Fenway (against the Angels), he sat and watched. At times, he must have privately wondered what on earth he was doing in Boston. As it turns out, he had been waiting to take his lead off first in the ninth inning of Game Four all along.

As he does, his small compact frame is crouched low to the ground with his left, trigger leg cocked toward second. Only thirty-two years old, Roberts's salt-and-pepper goatee gives the impression that he is significantly older. Perhaps it's a dupe into which suspect pitchers and catchers might fall, thinking the gray represents age, and that age represents deterioration, and that deterioration represents less than blistering speed. If this is the case, then Mariano Rivera is not among these suspect pitchers, for he nervously fires over a check on Roberts without so much as a glance to Bill Mueller at the plate. Roberts dives back, dusts himself off, and takes his lead. Rivera fires over again, and again Roberts dives back. Rivera takes the ball, comes set, then turns and fires once more, and once more Roberts dives back (close, this time). He stands, dusts himself off, and takes his lead.

Rivera comes set, looks in at Mueller, checks first, then fires home and the instant he does Roberts bursts from his stance toward second and sprints down the line, digging hard. He dives head-first, hands-first into second a second before Jeter's tag hits him on the arm. ($dr(x - y) < (r) + (s) + (n) + (7)!$) Safe. He pops off the bag and dusts himself off. As he does, the trade, the move, and the entire three months Dave Roberts patiently waited his turn on the bench have all become instantly justified and vitally significant.

## Part of the Story

The recorded history of baseball—the official record that is, the one of dusty books and brass plaques and somber documentaries—is filled with grand moments from the grand legends of the games. Surely the story of the 2004 Red Sox and their remarkable run through the playoffs will include more than a few of these grand moments. But its deeper, richer story—the one kept orally, by the fans who were there and some who were not, who relive and revive its characters and moments on snowy winter nights—will just as surely include room for each of the crucial steps that prepared the way for these more photogenic dramas.

Roberts's steal in Game Four, although it will certainly be mentioned in the story of the Sox historic ALCS comeback, has something of this local feel to it already, and one can gradually sense it slipping into the hands of the true historians of the game—the fans. In this sense, the image of Dave Roberts sprinting down the baseline and diving into second will truly live forever in the hearts and minds of Red Sox fans. Just for turning (>) into (<).

**idiot RULE:** *When asked to run, run fast. Run very, very fast.*

# His Day in the Sun

**On a long enough timeline,** every Red Sox player, no matter how minor his role in the history of the team, has his day in the Fenway sun. Tony Clark hit a home run on opening day at Fenway; Jeremy Giambi stole a crucial base to help beat the Yankees; and at the end of the 2003 season, when the Sox clinched their first playoff spot in four years, it was Ramiro Mendoza who was on the mound at the end to start the party. Even these general disappointments had their Fenway moments, as all Sox are bound to eventually.

And while Pokey Reese, the silky middle-infielder signed by the Sox in the winter of 2003, played a greater role in helping the Sox win than any of the above, injury (a torn ligament in his thumb) and overachievement (by Mark Bellhorn) relegated him to a more peripheral role than he was expected to play. No matter. His early work as the everyday shortstop and his late work as a defensive replacement at second, as well as the sparkling defense he displayed throughout, were more than enough to establish his importance to this championship season.

His role on the team was that of a versatile weapon (he played the role of Dave Roberts, and played it well, before the Sox acquired the real thing) who provided the small, almost imperceptible additions that separate a team of good players and a championship team. Yet, for all of this versatility, the place Pokey Reese ended up occupying in the hearts and minds of many Red Sox fans is a much more specific location, formed from a much more vivid memory, as any thoughts of Pokey Reese almost immediately take us back to that sunny Sunday afternoon at Fenway, May 8, 2004, and his moment in the sun.

## Po-Kee

The image—of Pokey Reese with a bat in his hands, in the batter's box—is so difficult for many to conjure that the memory begins with the ball shooting off the end of the bat, an 0-2 fastball from Kansas City's Jimmy Gobble that Reese has reached out and smacked on a line to right. As it skips on the outfield grass and scoots toward the line, Fenway cheers the single and shouts on the double—the ball rolling now as Reese rounds first and heads for second—a quick look over the shoulder, his thin arms holding a sprinter's form. Then, just before it reaches the wall, the ball takes a quick skip and hugs the wall (*excuse me*) past the onrushing Juan Gonzalez and goes deep into the right field corner. Reese sees it and digs hard around second, pushing now for third as Fenway rises and strains and glances from the ball to Reese to third base coach Dale Sveum, and when he waves his arm high and wide Fenway shouts louder as the ball comes lofting into the infield and Reese swings around third and heads for home—his arms wide now, head back, flailing down the stretch—to last long strides as the ball comes in and he dives to the plate and hits it with his left hand and instantly looks up—safe. Reese rolls over in the dirt with arms held wide, Johnny Damon standing just above him and already reaching down to pull him up.

Fenway, now silly with adoration, cheers him on more or less constantly through the next inning, until he comes up to bat again in the sixth, and the deep, full chants—Po-*Kee*, Po-*Kee*, Po-*Kee*—echo throughout Fenway as loud and as affectionate as for any of its legends. Two pitches later, Reese lifts an 0-1 sinker high over the Monster Seats in left for his second home run—one inside, one outside—of the afternoon. After a leisurely celebration lap around the bases, Pokey Reese sits in the Red Sox dugout as Fenway calls out to him, the loud chant continuing well past the at-bat. Finally, he answers it—rises to the top step of the dugout, and waves his helmet to the crowd—his moment in the Fenway sun complete.

## *Do you remember that game when . . .*

Pokey Reese could play ten seasons with the Red Sox and play a thousand games at Fenway, and yet when his name is mentioned around Sox fans, the image of his day—of him rolling in the dirt as Damon lifts him, of him standing on the top step, in the sun—would still not be far behind. We would still pause (thinking back, going back to that afternoon), and still say to one another, *Do you remember that game when he . . .*

And of course we would remember. And maybe after reliving it for a moment we would expand a bit, and say something about the crucial role he played filling in during the first half of the season, or about how comforting it was to be able to bring in a Gold Glove off the bench late in the game during the playoffs. But then, surely enough, we would drift back, and we would once again be in the sunny Fenway bleachers on that summer afternoon, and Pokey would be just now glancing back to see the ball shoot to the corner, and would just now cut second on his way to third, and we would rise to our feet again, and he would charge toward home again, and the whole wonderful joyous scene that followed would be there with us all over again, sunny as it ever was.

This is the power of the essential baseball moment, of the one instance when a player, any player, makes a name for himself in the hearts and minds of the fans with just one thrilling play, with just one wild sprint. That one play is all it takes to be remembered forever, as Reese always will so long as his name is still mentioned among fans, so long as we still turn to each other with a slight smile, and say, *I remember that game, that game when Pokey . . .*

**idiot RULE:** *Sometimes, it only takes one day to change everything.*

# Kapler Afield

**Watching the Sox** at home on the television, we see Gabe Kapler make three or four of the best catches of the season. They are each explosive, slashing dives across the outfield grass, stealing the ball with a flash of glove inches before it hits the ground as Kapler slides headfirst across the lawn, pops up, and fires the ball back into the infield. It is the kind of dashing outfield play that looks better with each and every slow-motion replay.

However, watching the Sox at Fenway from our seat in the right field grandstands, we witness something slightly different. We see the whole field, and because of this we see Kapler react to the ball off the bat with two quick, instinctive steps to his right; both in the wrong direction, as it turns out, since the ball is not hit quite as hard as he first judged it to be and is now falling fast in shallow right center. Kapler adjusts and sprints in, pushing hard and at the last instant leaps headfirst, headlong out over the grass and stretches his glove to sweep the ball out of the air inches from the grass as he goes crashing to the ground. It still looks good, is still an athletic, aggressive play and we still stand and applaud as Kapler, shaking grass from his belt, takes his place back in right; but, at the same time, we know that it did not have to be quite so fantastic.

## The Kapler Balance

But this then is Gabe Kapler as Sox fans have come to know him: an athletic, aggressive player who somehow lacks the essential baseball instincts to make him one of the game's special ones, but whose raw athletic talent and (more so) full-throttle style of play make him effective in any number of situations. In many ways, he is the exact opposite of Trot Nixon, the man he replaced in right field for much of the season, who, while not as strong or as fast, nonetheless possesses tremendous baseball instincts. (The irony being that Trot probably would have broken clean on the shallow fly, but lacking Kapler's speed, still would have had to dive to make the catch.) It is this play in the outfield, and several like it over the course of the season, which shows us perfectly both why Kapler is not in the everyday lineup and yet at the same time shows us why he managed to appear in nearly every Red Sox game of the season. His lack of natural baseball instincts failed him initially, and sent him two steps in the wrong direction, but his physical gifts and the fact that he plays every play of every game so damn hard balanced out this failure, and in the end he got the job done.

Signed as a midseason free agent in June of 2003 (after he was released by the Rockies), Kapler chose the Red Sox over a number of other interested teams because he wanted to be a part of a winner, despite the fact that he was almost certain to play less in Boston than elsewhere. With Manny, Damon, and Nixon, the Sox were set across the outfield, and could only use Kapler as a sometimes pinch hitter, sometimes pinch runner, sometimes defensive replacement, along with an occasional spot start against tough lefties. Kapler accepted, repeating that he wanted to play in a winning environment (his previous big league experience had been with Detroit, Texas, and Colorado), and signed on.

After a delirious Fenway debut against Florida, Kapler settled into his role until late in the season, when Nixon pulled a calf muscle and Kapler replaced him in right for the remainder of the year. The following April, when Nixon came into spring training with a back problem (which would later dovetail into a quad problem), Kapler once again stepped in. And although still not considered a regular, he played in 136 games during the regular season, including more in right field than any other player. He also appeared in all four World

Series games, coming on as a defensive replacement in right field to hold down the Sox lead.

## *MONSTER* minutiae

Kapler's presence in right field caused concern among fans in the bleachers, albeit for reasons completely unrelated to his play. When the Sox went to the bullpen mid-inning, Kapler jogged over to Johnny Damon in center, as outfielders often do during pitching changes, and the two stood shoulder to shoulder, talking. Meanwhile, the fans in the bleachers were treated to an ominous vision, with No. 18 Damon standing to the right of No. 19 Kapler—bold red numbers reading: 1918. Looking back, this numerology is somewhat amusing. Now

## Every Team Needs One

A muscular, wedge-shaped player with a wide smile and a customary day's worth of stubble, Kapler nearly always works (and overworks) a wad of gum in his right cheek, adding another twitch to his springy, almost hyper movements. Fast, strong, and agile, with good reflexes and a powerful throwing arm, he possesses every tool a baseball player needs except the one he cannot do without—instincts. Nowhere is this more evident than at the plate, where his constantly moving stance reminds one of a strong, fast decathlete having a go at the pole vault—he knows the technique, knows the motions, and has practiced relentlessly, but despite it all he still looks uncomfortable throughout the entire experience.

Why then did he play in 136 games over the course of the season? Why did he play in every World Series game? Why do Sox fans, on the whole, trust him in almost any position in almost any situation? The answer to all three is that Gabe Kapler plays the game as hard as anyone on the Sox team and maybe as hard as anyone in the game. In the outfield, he runs down every ball like it is the last out in the last game of the World Series. He throws every ball in as hard as he possibly can, often spinning himself off balance and to the ground in the process. He runs the basepaths relentlessly, ferociously, going first-to-third as well as anyone on the team, and almost never makes a mental mistake anywhere on the field. He is, quite simply, the kind of player you want on your team, and the kind of player every championship team needs and more often than not has. He is a gamer, a guy you want on the field when it comes down to it in the end—which is why he was on the Sox to begin with, and why he stayed, and why he was on the field when it came right down to it in the end.

**idiot RULE:** *It doesn't matter how you get there, just get there.*

# Part 2
## The Staff

# Professor Pedro and Mr. Martinez

*"Pedro is not 'some people.'"*
—Curt Schilling, during a call
he placed to WEEI, Sports Radio,
850 AM, on September 23, 2004

**Pedro Martinez** steps back onto
the mound at Camden Yards in
Baltimore on a frigid April night.
He presses his right foot to the
rubber and with his left shoulder to
the plate and glove at his side, raises
his right hand in a fist to his mouth and
blows one long breath into it as he looks
in toward the plate. Around him 47,683

Orioles fans clap thick mittens and cheer beneath black-and-orange sweatshirts and jackets, the full, gleeful sound of promise echoing down across the field and over the mound. On it, Pedro Martinez stands in his road gray uniform, tight and shiny red sleeves down his thin arms, silver chain around his collar, BOSTON in brilliant red letters across the front of his jersey, a bold no. 45 on the back with his name, MARTINEZ, arched above it.

# First Impressions

There is a thin strap of black across the bottom of his chin, and his curly black hair puffs out below the back of his cap, just a bit, covering the tops of his ears and nothing more. The expression on his face, mouth limp and eyes tired, gives away nothing of the situation surrounding him. With a nod, he brings ball to glove and comes set in a slight crouch—right knee bent, left leg locked and stretching out before him—and glances quickly at Larry Bigbie on third, who has recently reached base on a throwing error by Pedro (scoring Jay Gibbons, who had singled, from second); then quickly back over his left shoulder at Louis Matos on first, who has more recently singled to left on a change-up up in the zone, scoring David Segui (who had been hit by a pitch) from third. Sitting somewhere in the Baltimore dugout is Javy Lopez, who less recently led off the inning with a home run to left.

It is Opening Day, 2004. The score is 3-0, Baltimore. It is the second inning. There are no outs. And Pedro Martinez, standing set on the mound at Camden Yards on a frigid April night, is a man around whom there are many more questions than answers. Questions about his declining velocity (which has reached only the low-90s, and even then only occasionally, in spring training), questions about his declining greatness, questions about his declining effectiveness. Some say he is getting old and breaking down. Some say he is no longer the pitcher he once was and some say he never will be again; some say he is no longer a big game pitcher and some say he never was, anyway. Some say he is done.

But then Brian Roberts stands at the plate, and Pedro Martinez stands on the mound, and with Terry Francona in the dugout and the bullpen sitting silent, there is still another pitch to be thrown. And so Pedro Martinez looks in once more to Varitek, then kicks his left leg up quick and pushes off his right, and his hands break as the ball pulls out of the glove and his entire thin body whips forward as his left foot reaches up and out and . . . six and a half months later and 800 miles away, comes down on the mound in Busch Stadium as his shoulder drives down and whips the right arm through. The ball rockets home and pops into Varitek's mitt just before the sweep of Jim Edmonds's bat—for strike three.

## The Last Out

It is a pleasant October night in St. Louis, and as Edmonds walks back to the Cardinals dugout, Pedro Martinez circles the mound once before stepping back onto the rubber and looking in toward the plate. Around him, 52,015 Cardinals fans sit silently hunched forward in their red fleeces and sweatshirts, a dim ripple of muttering disappointment wavering in the background. On the mound, Pedro Martinez stands in his same road gray uniform, tight and shiny red sleeves down his thin arms, silver chain around his collar. This time, however, there is an oval aqua-and-black patch on the right sleeve of his jersey. The strap of black across the bottom of his chin is now wider and thicker, and his curly black hair hangs in limp wet strands down to his shoulders and sticks to the sides of his neck. The expression on his face, mouth limp and eyes tired, gives away nothing of the situation surrounding him. With a nod, he brings both ball and red glove up and holds it out away from his chin, staring over it—straight at Varitek. There is no one on his right, on third; there is no one behind him, on second; there is no one to his left, on first. It is Game Three of the 2004 World Series. The score is 4-0, Boston. It is the seventh inning. There are two outs. And Pedro Martinez, standing set on the mound at Busch Stadium on a mild October night, is a man with answers.

Yes, his velocity has declined by a degree, but only a degree (he was second in the league in strikeouts this season, with 227); and yes, he is getting older, but he is not yet breaking down (he did not miss a start all season); and yes, he is still effective (16 wins); and yes, now perhaps more than ever, he is still capable of greatness. In this, his first World Series start, he has allowed only three hits, and no runs over $6^2/3$, and with Edmonds on the bench has now retired twelve Cardinals in a row. But then Reggie Sanders still stands at the plate, and there is still another pitch to be thrown, and Pedro Martinez is not quite done, not yet.

## The Mr. Martinez Show

In the six and a half months and 800 miles between these two pitches, the Red Sox played 175 games, 137 of which found Mr. Martinez busy not on the mound, but in the dugout, usually on its top step and more usually talking—to the fans behind the Red Sox dugout, to his teammates in the dugout, to his teammates on the field, to himself, and anyone who would listen—waving his hands about across the field at a friend in the opposing dugout and hopping up and down on the top step for the final out of an inning.

We find him there now, on a warm midsummer night, warm-up sleeves hanging down to his hands and curly cloud of hair hanging from under a blue-and-red do-rag, *Dominican Republic* written on the band across his forehead. He holds a blue foam bat in his hands as he stands and takes an exaggerated stance on the dugout steps, crouched with hips swinging back and forth, waving the bat above his head as a visiting pitcher delivers to Manny Ramirez at the plate. Manny swings and crushes a breaking ball off the wall in left and sends Mr. Martinez dancing, hands over head and hips shaking. He stops and arches his back forward and laughing through a giant grin, thrusts both arms out and points the foam bat and his index finger to Manny on second. Manny points back and smiles.

## RED SOX NATION

Prior to Pedro, the best show in town was perhaps another great right-handed pitcher, Luis Tiant (1971–1978). It was Tiant's pitching that made him a Red Sox great, but it was always his vibrancy on the mound and off it that made him unforgettable. Unlike Pedro, though, Tiant's showmanship was on display almost wholly on the mound, where his unique wind-up and variety of peculiar deliveries became the show within the show every time he took the mound.

Another night, we find him there on the steps, this time seated and leaning one elbow on the top step, his head uncovered and dark curly afro glistening in the lights. He is wearing a pair of cheap, gold-rimmed, bug-eyed sunglasses (Elvis model, circa 1970). Another night, we find him at the end of the dugout, smiling with his arm around the tiny shoulders of a 36-inch-tall ceramic bobble-head doll of himself. Later in the season, we find him bounding off the top step into the dugout, smiling, to lean over Manny (who this time has crushed one over the wall in left) and shake his floppy black curls over Manny's head, the two laughing and slapping each other on the shoulder.

Welcome then, one and all, to the Mr. Martinez Show, now in its seventh season, playing all summer long at Fenway and around the American League. It is the product of one man's vision and energy and it is available for the entertainment of teammates, opposing teams, and fans all around the ballpark and at home by their televisions; but directed mostly (it seems) toward entertaining one man—the irrepressible Mr. Martinez himself. Because while this show goes on throughout the game and in front of all, it seems to have evolved not from an outward instinct to amuse others, but instead from a much more basic, much more internal instinct to amuse himself. After all, though the show may draw laughter and smiles and bewildered shakes of the head from teammates and fans alike, no one smiles wider than the man in the gold Elvis glasses, and no one laughs louder than the man who wags a foam bat and shakes his skinny ass on the top step of the Sox dugout.

# The Professor

Professor Pedro, however, does not smile. Instead, he works. He stands now on the mound in Angel Stadium on a warm early October night in southern California. With both ball and red glove held in front of his chin, he stares over the top edge of the glove. His eyes are still and his mouth slack and silent. It is Game Two of the ALDS. It is the seventh inning. The Sox lead the game 4-3 and the series 1-0. Professor Pedro has given up six hits and four runs and now faces Chone Figgins with two outs and none on. The count is 3-2. His next pitch to Figgins will be the tenth of the at-bat, and his 116th pitch of the night. It is the point in the game that some have said he no longer is able to finish. Some have said he no longer has the stuff.

Varitek calls for a change-up and Professor Pedro nods. He takes a short slide-step to the side, pivots, taps the right foot on the rubber, swings his left leg and arms up and back in one fluid swoop; then separates hand and ball from glove and pushes off. He drives forward and pulls his front shoulder down as his left leg stretches out, whips his right arm at a three-quarter angle across his body as he plants on the left foot and his entire body tilts to the left. His right leg and foot fly out to the right as the right arm bounces off the follow-through and swings back out, wide of the body as the pitch sails in—a fastball on the outside corner. Figgins swings through it, strikes out, and the inning ends. The fastball was clocked at 91 mph. Not great, but good enough.

Throughout the night it has reached as high as 94, and Professor Pedro has relied more heavily on his snap curveball (occasionally mixing in a slider or cutter), and his devastating change-up. He has good stuff—big time, big league stuff—still. Not the overpowering, supernatural stuff he was capable of throwing when he was twenty-six. But the motion and delivery are the same. The arm angle is still low and the whipping motion still a blur. The fastball still hits its mark and the bottom still falls out of the change-up. The old good stuff, though diminished a degree by time, is still there—still present within the slender right arm and the long, thin fingers.

## The Mr. Martinez Show: Q&A Period

Just ask him. Mr. Martinez will tell you. He will tell you the stuff is still there, and he will tell you he still has everything he needs to perform at the highest level of the game, and how he loves Boston, loves being a Bostonian, and wants to finish his career as a Red Sox, and then he will tell you that he is leaving, that this is his last year; and then he will go on to tell you that when he was a boy in the Dominican Republic he used to wait outside in the shade of a mango tree, waiting for the bus, a poor kid with nothing to his name and nothing to look forward to, and how he feels lucky to be here. Then, just as soon as he is done telling you this, he will tell you how he wants a ring now, a big diamond World Series ring, how the time is right in his career and he wants it now, this year; but then, before you go, he will tell you he is not talking to you anymore.

Listen closely to what he says, and if you have a tape recorder on you it might be a good idea to keep it running, because this is the Mr. Martinez Show Q&A Period and you never know what he might say tonight. Over the past seven seasons, the various reporters and journalists who cover the Red Sox, and are therefore privy to the Q&A segment of the Mr. Martinez Show, have come to learn two lessons:

1. Listen and record every word Mr. Martinez says because he is one of the most intelligent and articulate players on the team, and . . .
2. Take nothing Mr. Martinez says literally without thorough inspection of tone, context, and purpose, because he is one of the most intelligent and articulate players on the team.

This Q&A time is a game show, a psychological shell game that continues on throughout the season whether both sides decide to play or not (and whether or not both sides even know when they're playing). One side points to a shell and asks, *Are you intimidated by the Yankee tradition?* The other side (the host) picks up an empty shell and says, *Wake up the damn Bambino . . . maybe I'll drill him in the ass.* Try again. The shells are shuffled, set in place, and one side points to a shell and asks, *Why is it you seem to be struggling so much against the Yankees?* The other side picks up an empty shell and says, *I just tip my hat and call the Yankees my daddy.* Sorry, try again. The shells are reshuffled, set in place. Frustrated now, one side points to a shell and asks, *What does this all mean to you going from start to finish this year?* The other side smiles, picks up a shell, points to a big shiny diamond ring beneath it, and says, *I hope everybody enjoyed it as much as I did.*

## The Professor at the Podium

Professor Pedro, however, says nothing. He stands on the mound at Fenway Park on a cool, crisp autumn evening with the ball in his hand, facing in at Yankees shortstop Derek Jeter. It is Game Five of the ALCS. It is the fourth inning. The Sox lead 2-1 in the game and trail 3-1 in the series. Professor Pedro is not playing games; he is lecturing. He stares in over the top of his red glove and the eyes and mouth are silent and still, without expression and without emotion.

It is the same focused, determined look he gave hitters a decade earlier in Montreal. It is the same look he gave hitters when he arrived at Fenway in 1998. And it is the look we at Fenway and we at home have watched for the past seven seasons as Professor Pedro has stared back at us in the ballpark and through our television screens. Some say it is meant to intimidate. Others say it is born of concentration. Still others say it is a control device, meant to block out the thousands of distractions swirling throughout the ballpark and hone the focus down to one precise point within the strike zone. It is, it seems, a combination of each of these elements and yet a product of none of them.

Watching Professor Pedro on the mound, looking back at him as he looks out at his catcher, what we see is exactly what we would expect to see: a man locked in competition. This confrontation between pitcher and hitter (unlike the more jovial and casual encounters between press and pitcher) is no psychological shell game. Instead, we see two men playing chess and arm wrestling at the same time. The mind and body simply have no room for anything else; and so nothing else is expressed, nothing else is exposed. The pitcher looks at the catcher, makes a move on the chessboard, then buckles down to pull the arm over the top. As he does, as the pitch is delivered, the expression changes; the lower lip juts out and the eyes bulge wide open, the look suddenly pure effort, expressive and exposing. Focus and force, the two looks of Professor Pedro show us nothing and everything—the concentrated meditation on how to pitch, followed by the explosive release of the pitch itself (the two, together, are what we call pitching). But there is a third look. The same as the first in silence, the same as the second with its driving, penetrating stare. We have seen it exactly once, at Yankee Stadium on September 19, 2004. That afternoon, Professor Pedro gave up seven hits and eight runs. When he was pulled without recording an out in the sixth he began a long, slow walk across the infield to the visitors' dugout. As he did, 55,000 howling Yankees fans rained down a Stadium-shaking wall of noise, riding him, step by step as he walked under a hail of derision—shouts and calls mocking him from the closer rows, and signs taunting him.

It was one of the single most humiliating and degrading moments of his long, distinguished career, and he never looked down. He never bowed his head. Not once. From the rubber to the dugout, and every step of the way, he held his stare on the crowd, faced its every point and listened to its every shout. On the top step of the visitors' dugout, he paused just a moment, head held up, and looked unblinking into the crowd. Embarrassed, shamed, and humbled, he never dipped his eyes. It was one of the proudest moments of his career.

## The Mr. Martinez & Nelson Blowout Victory Extravaganza

A prouder moment, we may assume, was the celebration that followed thirty-eight days later in the visiting club at Busch Stadium, after the Sox won the World Series and Mr. Martinez secured his big fat diamond ring. This moment is probably only slightly prouder than the moment back in Yankee Stadium a week earlier, where Mr. Martinez celebrated an American League championship as the same Yankees fans who taunted him filed out silently above. And this moment is probably only slightly prouder than the scene back at Fenway eleven days earlier, where Mr. Martinez celebrated an ALDS sweep by strapping a pair of swimming goggles over his eyes, putting a plastic bucket on his head, and hoisting Nelson de la Rosa, a 29-inch-tall Dominican man, high into the air. Drenched in champagne and beer, goggles over eyes and bucket on head, these celebrations brought out the best, the brightest, and the loudest in Mr. Martinez—all the laughter and playfulness of his dugout dancing and all the humor and wit of his postgame statements, all soaked in champagne and accompanied by his tiny virtuoso sidekick.

## MONSTER minutiae

Nelson first arrived in the Red Sox clubhouse in September, as a guest of Mr. Martinez. The Sox hit a hot streak right around that time, and Mr. Martinez declared Nelson the team's good luck charm (and, unofficially, the co-host of the Mr. Martinez Show). From then on, he became a regular sight around the team. It says something of the peculiarities in a clubhouse that contained the likes of Millar, Damon, Manny, and Ortiz, that a 29-inch-tall singing-and-dancing Dominican man was a fairly normal and not particularly notable sight. In a Sox clubhouse that was often described as a 25-ring circus, he fit right in.

*Step inside, step inside, to the show that never ends*, it is the Mr. Martinez & Nelson Blowout Victory Extravaganza, a wild night of jokes and pranks, of singing and dancing, of high wit and low humor—the most amazing, fun-filled hour-and-a-half in baseball and it all comes to you live and in vibrant color on three different nights in October. It is wild, it is crazy, it is senseless and sensational, it makes you laugh and smile and shake your head, and you will never see another performance like it as long as you follow the game—it is the incomparable madness of Mr. Martinez.

## The Master Lecture

But before this last show, Professor Pedro has to finish the job (he is not quite done, not yet). He stands on the mound in Busch Stadium on a mild October night with two outs in the seventh inning. Reggie Sanders stands at the plate. The count is 1-2. At this moment, Professor Pedro—his stringy black hair hanging down from his hat, strands sticking to his neck, the silver chain around his collar and red glove held in front of him—is still at work. He stares in.

The concentrated meditation he and Jason Varitek conduct on how to pitch Reggie Sanders shifts another piece across the chessboard (meanwhile, we get the impression Sanders has blinked, and hardly notices anything different about the board that has just tilted against him), and Professor Pedro adjusts his long fingers across the ball in his glove. The entire deliberation process between he and Varitek has taken approximately fifteen seconds. And yet this process continues to makes Professor Pedro effective; continues to push him to greatness. Long after the velocity on his fastball deteriorates for good, and long after the arm strength has shortened his outings and innings, the intelligence behind the still and silent look will continue to bring about greatness on the mound. Earlier in his career, when the fastball was overpowering and the stuff electric, the intelligence made this greatness legendary, but now, later on, when age and innings have dulled the vibrancy of the pitcher's raw tools, it has been the intelligence that has proved the most invaluable of all tools (the only one that does not dull with time and use).

The transitional period between these two stages of a career stretched between the end of the 2003 season and the early months of 2004, and the struggles that came along with it were both blatantly obvious and painfully public. Some saw this, and said he was done. (Another empty shell is turned. *Sorry, try again.*) But he was not done, not yet. His mind reassessed the tools at its disposal, rearranged its way of approaching hitters, and stepped back onto the mound. This type of evolution, this adaptation, is the outward sign of superior intelligence that Professor Pedro has shown throughout his career, but perhaps displayed in its purest form during the 2004 season, culminating in his final start and crystallized in his final inning of work.

Yet he still, now, has one pitch left to throw. His grip set, he steps back, taps the right foot, separates and drives forward, whips the arm through and fires—a hard fastball blazing past the late swing of Sanders—strike three. The inning and the outing are over. Professor Pedro steps off the mound and points with both fingers to the sky, glancing up as he does, and walks across the infield to the dugout. He has just pitched a seven-inning, three-hit shutout. It is his first World Series start. It is his first World Series win. It is the greatest lecture he has ever given, a Ph.D.-level dissertation delivered to the perfect audience at exactly the right time. It has been his masterpiece, his legacy—the definitive account of the genius of Professor Pedro.

## Not "Some People"

Curt Schilling once said, memorably, "Pedro is not 'some people.'" He was right. In the dugout, Pedro is not even like other ballplayers, his playfulness during off games the kind of lighthearted mischievousness that is suppressed even in little league dugouts, much less the top step of the Sox dugout at Fenway. His curious, often mystifying dialogues with the press display a wit and wisdom (not always in equal parts) that simply are not often found in combination, either in baseball or any other area of life. Together, it is a kind of exuberant madness, and it is almost impossible to turn away from.

On the days he pitches, he stands on the mound unlike any other. Combining tremendous talent with superior intelligence (not, as some often say, merely *baseball* intelligence, but intelligence, period) he has continued to dominate because he has continued to adapt, and because of this he is still capable of greatness—especially when greatness is called for. This adaptation—the way his intelligence has carried him across from talent to trade—represents a kind of genius, and it too is nearly impossible to turn from.

So, which is the true Pedro Martinez? Is he Mr. Martinez—the dancing clown, shaking his hips on the top step of the dugout? Or is he Professor Pedro—leveling a silent stare over his red glove? Yes. Yes, he is. He is both; both the skinny man bouncing through the dugout, shaking his hair over Manny Ramirez's head, and the intimidating Hall of Famer staring down from the mound. Yes, he is both the explosive eyes-bulging delivery in the bottom of the seventh and the goggled, bucket-covered celebration in the clubhouse after the game. He is all of these things and no less, no less than both a clown and a legend, no less than a madman and a genius—no less than the one and only Pedro Martinez.

**idiot RULE:** *Don't mistake the show for the showman.*

# Chapter 10

# Curt ex machina

**There is a reason** why there is so little good baseball fiction—why the majority of it tends to be either far too predictable (the young rookie pitcher struggling, overcoming, winning the big game in the end) or, worse, far too unpredictable and therefore far too unbelievable, too unacceptable to the baseball audience who understands the game and its possibilities, and will therefore not tolerate those possibilities being taken advantage of by some *artiste*.

When a baseball audience sees a fastball clocked at 130 mph, sees the weak-hitting rookie hit a towering grand slam, or sees the pitcher who broke his arm in Act I come into the big game in Act III, our immediate reaction is to roll our eyes, fold our arms over our chests, sigh a heavy *hurumph,* and shake our heads. The elegant intricacies of the game have been violated by some director who, failing to come up with a plausible outcome, has resorted to a ploy, has crammed an implausible outcome into the story without regard to the game or the audience.

## Advance Billing

The key to keeping this from happening is to create an interesting and complex set of problems for the characters/players—some situation for which there seems no positive resolution (say, for example, being down 3-0 in a best-of-seven series, with the star pitcher needing season-ending surgery). Then a solution is presented that is both engaging and interesting but, at the same time, believable within the bounds of possibility. The key, then, to really good baseball fiction is to surprise a baseball audience without breaking the restraints of plausibility. The reason why there is so little good baseball fiction is because it has to compete with baseball reality—upon which there are no such restraints.

As baseball fans then, we can sympathize with the producer of baseball fiction because we know as well as any how difficult this job of creating plausible resolutions can be. We know because we do it ourselves—every season, every game. Every time we find our team in some awful bases-loaded, nobody-out situation (the game tied, our starter out of gas, our bullpen racing to get warm, and the opposing slugger stepping to the plate), we go through the exact same process of producing baseball fiction, and ask ourselves the exact same question—*How on earth do we get out of this mess?* We sit down, look at the situation, look at the characters we have to work with, and ask ourselves—*All right, how do I make a happy ending out of this?* It is the question every baseball fan poses internally each and every spring, and as in baseball there is only *one* happy ending for *one* team each season the question becomes simplified even further, and we ask ourselves—*How, plausibly, could this team win the World Series?*

Of course, we can only watch the same production with the same outcome (regardless of changes in cast) so many times without having to find some new conflict. As Red Sox fans, knowing the production by heart, we came up with a new question. We ask it each March as spring training begins and our cast is assembled, as costumes are handed out and rehearsals begin on a play that has not yet been written. We ask it every spring, and we asked it in the spring of 2004, as the Red Sox gathered in Fort Myers—*What is it, specifically, that makes this year different from any other in our lifetime?*

# Act I

The answer, in bold letters across the top of our 2004 Red Sox playbill, was the man who had been cast as the hero—Curt Schilling. This was how the story was billed: The Red Sox team that came within five outs of the World Series returns for the new season with the same basic roster, but has added a closer and, more significantly, a big, confident, experienced starter at the top of the rotation. This starter, the hero, steps in and performs brilliantly all season long; he works hard, wins games, and helps get the team back to the ALCS; and, once there, the hero makes the difference—he is the one who makes up those last five outs, he is the one element that was missing, the one addition that will make the difference. He is, quite simply, the answer to the question, *Why will the Red Sox win the World Series this year?*

Curt Schilling is the solution. He is the resolution to the mess of problems Red Sox fans have been looking for a way out of their entire lives, the one character and one plot twist that will turn tragedy into epic. This, of course, was how the story was billed in March, and this was the performance Sox fans believed themselves to be settling in for on Opening Day, when the curtain rose on Act I of the 2004 season. As it turned out, this first act was a bit of a clunker—full of muddled casting and slowed by awkward, and at times bewildering stage direction—but it wrapped up with something of a flourish. We saw a handful of brisk, late-summer scenes where the whole cast seemed to finally be on the same page, the action lively and promising.

## First Intermission

By the time we all settled back into our seats after the first intermission and prepared ourselves for Act II (the ALCS), there was a quiet (and at times not-so-quiet) confidence that this production was going exactly as planned. Curt Schilling had performed brilliantly all season and helped bring the Sox back to the ALCS, where he took the mound for Game One and seemed poised to fulfill his own advanced billing, prepared to answer the eternal Red Sox question and become the difference between this season and each of the 86 that had preceded it. The stage was set, the lights came on, and when the curtain rose there he was, center stage—Curt Schilling, the hero.

# Act II

Then, the script changed. With two outs in the bottom of the first, Gary Sheffield doubled. Then Hideki Matsui doubled (1-0) and Bernie Williams singled (2-0). In the third, Matsui doubled with the bases loaded (5-0) and Jorge Posada added a sacrifice fly (6-0). Sox fans, as an audience, shuffled in our seats, twisted our programs, tried to remain calm. As bad as these scenes looked, as miserable as the prospect of losing Game One seemed, the situation was certainly not desperate, not yet. This was simply conflict, as much a part of postseason baseball as any other good drama. If the Red Sox and Schilling were to give a good story, a good ending, they would overcome it. *Don't worry*, we said, *this is just part of the story.*

But then Schilling limped a bit stepping back on the mound. Something about his delivery looked odd—more upright and reluctant than usual, unsure of itself. First the announcers, and then we too, whispered a shattering word, slipping through the theater. *He looks*, we said in disbelief, *injured.* We watched as he gingerly stepped off the Yankee Stadium mound after the third, his night finished. As the word was repeated the following morning, and the details of the injury were revealed, this worry grew into a kind of numb despair. When the Sox lost Game Two the following evening, this numbness wore off and we became genuinely upset. Two nights later, after Schilling was all but ruled out for the season and the Sox were destroyed by the Yankees in Game Three, our suspension of belief finally cracked and crumbled before us and we, as Sox fans, panicked.

## Second Intermission

*This isn't right*, we said to each other, *this is not how this story was supposed to go. Schilling was supposed to be the answer, he was supposed to be the difference and now he's done for the year? How is that possible? Is this the right play? Am I even at the right theater?* We unfold our crumpled playbills and point to the title. *Yes, see, right there, across the top*: The 2004 Season, The Year the Red Sox Win the World Series; *and here* (turning to the back), *right at the top of the cast list*: Curt Schilling, the Hero.

You see, he was the reason we all arrived so hopeful in the first place; he was the reason we patiently waited through that first, plodding act of a regular season; and he was the reason we were led to believe that this production, this year, was not the same tragedy we had watched over and over again every season of our lives, but instead something new and different—a revival of a dusty legend called A Red Sox Championship. Sox fans bought into this advertisement from the very beginning, ate it up, and through the regular season as the Sox struggled and the Yankees took their place at the top of the division, it was the promise of Curt Schilling in October that extended our best hopes of change despite the fact that, by all appearances, nothing had actually changed at all.

These hopes were invested almost wholly in the idea of Curt

Schilling on the mound in Game One of the ALCS, in Yankee Stadium, and nothing that went wrong during Act I—the injuries to key position players, a struggling third starter, the atrocious defense, questionable managing, or even a ten-game deficit to the Yankees—could shake these beliefs, so strongly were they supported by the sturdy image of Curt Schilling standing tall on the mound. When he fell, the whole show—cast, costume, set, and stage—came crashing down around him. And now, out in the hallway during the second intermission, we can hardly bring ourselves to return to our seats; and it is only with a deep breath that we finally, begrudgingly and despondently, shuffle back into the theater and slump back into our seats.

Down 3-0, the Hero having exited the stage limping, the weather cool and the sky gray, we shake our heads and wonder: *How on earth do we get out of this mess?* The story has changed, and we need a new ending. But how? Even if we were to win Game Four, and even if we were to win Game Five, who would pitch in Game Six? We can only work with the characters we're given, and at the moment we're down exactly one Hero. To introduce another at this point seems unlikely, seems too implausible, and we are neither drunk enough, or foolish enough, or childish enough to indulge in this or similar fantasies. It does us no good to drift off thinking about an unknown reliever miraculously stepping up and pitching a no-hitter, or our bats suddenly catching fire and putting up 25 runs every single game, or even the entire Yankees roster suddenly falling violently ill and requiring hospitalization (an absurd suggestion, made in complete earnestness at the time).

No, none of these daydreams will do. We know the game, and we know its limitations, and we will not allow ourselves to let faith degenerate into delusion. We will not allow ourselves to be made a fool of, not again. But still, we need an ending. So we settle in as the curtain rises on the second act, and think: *How, plausibly, could this story find a happy ending?*

## deus ex machina

It is a shame that the story we are watching is not a classical Greek drama. If it were, we could count on one of Greek drama's favorite means of resolving such complex problems, which was to wheel one of its gods onto the stage with a machine. The Greek playwrights, finding their plots insufferably complicated and their characters not up to the task of resolving their own dire problems, created resolution by writing a deity into the final act, usually brought on stage by means of a machine (levers and pulleys, carts and such). This god solved all mortal problems in a few quick lines and just like that, *happily ever after*, the play ended. The technique is known as *deus ex machina* (literally, "God from a machine") and quickly fell out of fashion with modern playwrights and audiences who, for one thing, no longer believed much in Greek gods but were also no longer willing to believe in such contrived, manipulative endings in their dramas. Believability became a vital element in the construction of engaging plots, and there has been very little good baseball fiction ever since.

Modern audiences simply reject any hint of deus ex machina trickery, just as modern baseball fans reject wide-eyed, dreamy delusions such as, *Well, if we just hit two grand slams, and then get a few guys on base . . . maybe*, or, *If every player on our roster has a career year, and every team in our division suffers key injuries then, maybe. . . .* We will have none of it. The game of baseball has its limitations and boundaries—we know this from experience, from having been too often fooled. If a solution is to be found, it must (as it must in art) come from within those bounds and within those limitations. This, then, is where we look for resolution as we settle in and watch the first, thrilling scenes of our third act.

## Act III, Scenes 1 and 2

Game Five at Fenway (Act III, scene 1), provides fantastic drama, as does Game Six (Act III, scene 2). We notice as we edge up in our seats, closer to the stage, that both have provided breathtaking excitement and intrigue within the boundaries of the game itself. They have pushed the very limits of belief and were, at the same time, believable within the context of the story. The acquisition of Dave Roberts for his speed on the basepaths set up his steal in Game Five; Bill Mueller's dramatic home run off Rivera in late July (back in Act I), set up his game-tying hit later on (in Act III); David Ortiz's heroic series-winning home run in the ALDS set up his ALCS heroics; and so on.

As dramatic as this all is, it still makes sense—it is wonderful and gripping drama, but it is still baseball drama as we know it, as we have come to understand it from a lifetime of study.

Yet at this point, waiting for the next scene to unfold, we still have not resolved the most troubling of our problems—replacing the vacated role of the Hero. What then, will happen next? Who will it be? An unheralded reliever? A starter going on a couple of days' rest? As enthralled with this drama as we are, we could believe almost anything, anything at all. So we twist our programs in our hands once again, and lean forward in our seats—and just then, if we are not mistaken, we hear a slight clicking noise coming from somewhere off-stage, strange mechanical sounds, like the gears of a machine.

## Act III, Scene 3

The scene begins. The Hero steps on stage, and we stare up in utter disbelief. Curt Schilling, a week removed from walking off the Yankee Stadium mound defeated and debilitated, now stands behind that same mound. His back to home plate, his left hand holding his blue hat to his chest and his right hand holding the small gold pendant on a chain around his neck to his mouth, he presses it to his lips as he mutters a private, concentrated prayer. He tucks the small pendant under his jersey, pulls on his hat, and turning around, steps onto the mound in the center of Yankee Stadium, glove on hand, ball in glove. He is tall and as top-heavy as ever, with a thick chest and broad shoulders. He wears long red sleeves under his gray jersey and pants down to within a few inches of his cleats, with a few inches of white socks showing on thin, stalky ankles.

The game begins when he blows on his right hand, brings his black glove up in front of his chin, and rests his right hand within it, looking in to catcher Jason Varitek, then nods and steps back. At this moment we, the audience, suddenly become intensely, acutely aware of the motion and delivery we have become familiar with throughout the season. We study it, compare it to the ideal in our mind.

He steps back and to the left, as normal, ball held in glove away from his chest, then pivots, taps the right foot, brings glove and ball up over his head, back behind the hat, and back down to the hips as the left knee rises and the shoulders turn, and waits a beat. Then the right hand pulls the ball out and down, dropping it to the right hip as the shoulders turn, the right leg drives out, and the front shoulder pulls down and carries the right arm up and over and into the long, smooth follow-through. The ball darts in for a called strike, and we shake our heads—the motion exactly how we pictured it.

Schilling gets the ball back, steps to the rubber, and repeats. Step and throw. Then again. One out; two outs; three outs. First inning; second inning; third inning. Every inning, every out, every pitch, is a remarkable event in our experience as baseball fans—this, whatever this is, simply does not happen. And yet it is happening.

Schilling had chosen to undergo an experimental surgery that we did not quite, at the moment, understand. Now he stands on the mound and labors slowly, deliberately, through each and every pitch—still favoring it, still testing—cautiously measuring out each delivery. And as he does, we notice something there, on his right ankle, that we have never seen before in a baseball game. The television cameras pan in on the white sock just above his black cleat, spotted now with a large blot of damp red blood. It is a fixating image.

Through it, he continues to pitch, one pitch at a time. Between innings, the scene shifts, and we see (if we are watching on television) an even more gripping image of Schilling. He sits in the Red Sox dugout—jacket on and rubbing his blond hair and the sides of his damp face with the thick white towel, then gripping his head, by the sides, with the towel over it, then holding it to his mouth, his eyes frantic above the towel as he stares out at the field—the sight of a man mentally rallying himself, anguishing with the expectations he holds himself to and the challenge he finds himself entangled within. It is an image of electric human drama.

## *MONSTER* minutiae

Credit would be given here (if this were fiction) to costume design for this ingenious device, for it added the last, crucial detail to the scene. As clever playwrights have long known, audiences need some bit of tangible proof whenever a physical device is used in the plot—and the more astounding the plot twist, the more necessary it is to include it. If the character has been shot in the arm, there should be blood, or at least a bandage. Similarly, those watching Game Six of the ALCS could be told how injured Schilling was and that he had been cut open in order to pitch, but these words would only do so much, and imagination had to do the rest. The bloody sock cleared the need for additional words or imagination by showing us. There it is, right in front of you: This man is bleeding.

The sight of it and of Schilling's return to the mound and each of his labored, measured deliveries hereafter causes us to fall back in our seats. Our jaws drop open as the program slips from our hands to the ground, rendered utterly speechless and in complete awe of the moment.

## The Curt *ex machina* Moment

The solution to our intricate and twisted plot was not, as it turns out, available for us to find because it was not within the bounds of our baseball reality. It came from somewhere else, a *deus ex machina* in the third act that we never saw coming because we had never seen it before, or anything like it. This surprise, this Curt *ex machina* in

Game Six of the ALCS, was conceived and executed offstage and unbeknownst to us through the genius of the physician/playwright Dr. Bill Morgan, the Red Sox team doctor. (The plot twist might then more accurately be known as the Curt *ex* Dr. Morgan technique).

Dr. Morgan had to explain it to us, later on—how the tendon that had become dislocated in Schilling's ankle had to be moved aside and sutured to the bone of his ankle, which was then stitched shut. We blink. We nod. *Okay, well, did not see that coming; nope, not at all.* And so we give ourselves over to the story, let our programs lie on the ground beneath our seats and simply watch. There are no boundaries left after Game Six, no limits to the reaches of baseball drama—and with that we give up our predicting, and simply make ourselves comfortable, sit back, and enjoy the rest of the show.

## The Encore

Like all great performers after all great performances, Schilling knows how to give an encore—knows that it must both live up to and in some ways exceed the show itself. Five days later, when he takes the mound at Fenway for Game Two of the World Series, he gives the encore of a lifetime. Working even more carefully, limping even more tenderly as he tests the ankle off the mound, he painstakingly labors through 94 pitches, each one adding acclaim to his story as Fenway cheers his every movement. He works through six innings, pausing at times on the mound to collect himself before moving on, taking deep breaths and short, careful steps.

In the end, he walks off with the Sox leading (4-1) in the game and about to go up 2-0 in the Series. As we rise and applaud his exit before the final curtain with a full, deep ovation, we glance down at our playbills, crumpled at our feet. We see its title and advance billing, then turn back to the man himself as he tips his cap and exits into the Red Sox dugout. With that, we realize we have arrived at the right theater and the right play after all, that yes, this is: The 2004 Season, The Year the Red Sox Win the World Series; and yes, Curt Schilling is the Hero.

## The Reviews

There are actually several reasons why there is very little good baseball fiction, and chief among them may be because it is so very hard to believe in characters such as Curt Schilling. As modern audiences, we tend to scoff at such blunt, unapologetic heroes who step up in Act I and tell us that everything is going to be all right because of them and then, later on in Act III, make everything all right by riding in on a white horse and saving the day. We tend to prefer our heroes just a bit more complicated, a bit more flawed, and a bit more human. They are more believable that way.

And similarly, we do not often appreciate being surprised by such *deus ex machina*–type stunts as experimental surgery. We would rather the plot be resolved from within, with some known outcome that we can carefully piece together from the story preceding it (we would rather react by saying, *ahh, I see*, than, *wait, what?*). The story is more believable that way.

But Curt Schilling is not a character, he is a pitcher. And his accomplishments in Game Six of the ALCS and Game Two of the World Series are not fiction, they are reality. He signed with the Red

Sox with the clearly stated purpose of helping them overcome the Yankees and win the World Series. He made no apologies for this goal, made no concessions to its historical difficulties. (He did not come to try and maybe give the team a chance to one day, possibly, have a shot at winning; but instead, he stated that he was here to win the whole thing, this year.) He worked and pitched at the highest level through the entire season, and broke down only when his body physically gave out from beneath him. And yet, facing season-ending surgery and an offseason of waiting, he was given the option of experimental surgery and took it, risking the game, series, season, and possibly his career. He overcame tremendous physical and even greater mental obstacles in order to do exactly what he promised to do on the day he arrived in Boston: help the Red Sox overcome the Yankees and go on to win the World Series.

That is the reality of Curt Schilling. And although we may shake our heads and disbelieve such grand characters when they appear in art, when they appear in life, we recognize them for what they are, as heroes; and although in fiction we may not believe such impossible feats as his performance in the 2004 postseason, when it unfolds before us we recognize it as a story that goes beyond belief, beyond plausibility, and beyond the borders of our previous baseball reality, and we know this type of baseball story is not a story at all—but a legend.

**idiot RULE:** *There are no rules.*

# Chapter 11

# Old Socks, New Socks

## Old Sox

**For Sox fans,** Wakefield is
different. In our minds he
occupies a unique space,
and we speak of him with
a different tone than the
rest—more familiar, more famil-
ial. Whereas Johnny Damon's presence
in center field is greeted by the bleachers
with the excitable shouts of a rock star
reception (*Johnny! Johnny!*), and David
Ortiz's name ringing out over the loudspeakers and his presence lumbering to
the plate is greeted by all of Fenway

with a deep, almost worshiping gratefulness (*Awww, yeah, Big Papi!*), the reception we give Tim Wakefield is different. Quite different.

As he steps from the dugout and walks across the Fenway grass on his way to the bullpen, and the fans in even the farthest reaches of the bleachers (way back there, under the scoreboard) recognize the upright shape and the tiny, bird-toed steps, the reaction is oftentimes only a slight nod, with quieter, more reserved applause and a calmer, more respectful salute. (*Ah, Wake. Good to see you, buddy.*) No one shouts, no one jumps up and down and runs to the front ledge and waves their hands wildly. Instead, each fan politely claps and gives a short nod to the man, who before he reaches the bullpen door gives a low salute with his hand up, head still down at his feet. We realize in this moment that an understanding, something old and unspoken, has just been exchanged between fan and player—that a very old pact has just been renewed. The reception Fenway gives Wakefield—the upright, reserved applause we give him, and the quick, low wave he gives us—feels more common and more everyday than the red carpet treatment most Sox players receive, somehow less fussy and hurried, with all the familiarity, respect, appreciation, genuine care between both parties summed up and reaffirmed in this one basic, quiet exchange. Like a firm handshake between two very old friends.

## We Go Way Back . . .

The reason for this, or at least part of it, is because Sox fans have been shaking hands with Tim Wakefield (and he with us) longer than any other current Red Sox player—far longer. Wake arrived in Boston in

1995 during a now-distant era of Red Sox baseball in which the Sox as a team were on the cusp, just showing signs, of putting together the pieces that would eventually become the 2004 World Champions. But not quite yet.

Red Sox baseball, circa 1995—Greenwell and Mo and Johnny V (at short), Clemens and Lee Smith and Jeff Suppan (v. 1.0), and even Eric Hanson and Tim Naehring and Vaughn Eshelman—was still grounded in the cramped, dark corridors of old Fenway Park, and the faces and names who would transform both the organization and the ballpark were still scattered across the country, just starting off down the roads that would eventually lead them all to Boston. Keith Foulke was in San Jose. Bill Mueller was in Shreveport and Kevin Millar was in Brevard County. Johnny Damon was in Wichita, a few months away from his major league debut in Kansas City, and Jason Varitek was in his first professional season in the Mariners' system at Port City, where he met and caught a young pitcher named Derek Lowe. Ortiz was in Peoria and Trot was in the Sox organization, but still in A-ball in Sarasota, and Kevin Youkilis was still back in Cincinnati, still in high school, a month away from getting his driver's license. Pedro was struggling to find his form in Montreal and Schilling was struggling in Philadelphia.

During that first season, only one brief glimpse of the future would cross Wake's path, when in Game Three of the 1995 ALDS he stepped to the mound and looked in at an explosive young outfielder for Cleveland named Manny Ramirez. But the impression was brief (the Sox were swept) and unremarkable (Manny went 0-12 in the series), and the two parted ways as Wake took the loss and Manny went on to play in his first World Series, losing it a decade before he would win both it and its MVP award.

It took the better part of nine years and thousands upon thousands of miles to bring these various names and faces together in the Red Sox clubhouse at Fenway, but during all that time, Tim Wakefield never moved—he never needed to. He was already here, all that time (around 1450 Sox games in all), arriving at the ballpark, pulling on his longsleeve mock-turtlenecks (first blue, then red) and buttoning up his white No. 49 Sox jersey, pulling on his blue Sox hat and lacing up his cleats, walking out onto the Fenway grass and taking tiny, bird-toed steps to the bullpen. Each time the crowd gives him his polite welcome cheer (*hey'ya, Tim, how's it going*), and he gives us a low salute (*hey, guys, good to see ya*) in response.

Which brings us back to that handshake.

## One of Us

Perhaps among no other fan culture is time more of an issue than among Red Sox fans, for whom the acceptance or denial of time's significance is an issue of continual debate (even now), and among whom authority on time is only recognized through experience, only measured in years. It is poor form for those who have been at Fenway for only two seasons to try and tell those who have been there for twenty something about time. This type of presumption is greeted, at best, with indifference. (*You weren't there, you don't understand.*)

This is why so many Sox fans have difficulty when our newly acquired middle reliever, or our fresh-from-Pawtucket rookie attempts to explain something of the Red Sox experience, something of its past; and it is why we shift in our seats and cross our arms and grumble when the network announcer—rushed in on a flight from Los Angeles with his suitcase sitting behind him in the broadcast booth—tries to tell us about suffering. Sox fans simply do not want to hear it, not from other fans around the league, not from announcers from around the networks, and most of the time not even from our own players—none of whom were there, either.

CURSE BUSTERS

Wake was there in '95 when the Sox were swept by the Indians; he was there in '98 when they lost to them again; he was there in '99 when they overcame the Indians in five dramatic games, only to lose to the Yankees in five more; he was there in '00 when the Sox fell 2½ games short and missed the playoffs; and he was there in '01 when the whole thing fell apart; he was there in spring training of '02 when the Sox tried for a fresh start with a brand-new manager; and he was there two years later, in '04, when they tried again.

But Wake *was* there. He has experienced every win and every loss, every shining moment of personal achievement and every embarrassing moment of nonsense, every promising new addition and every disappointing new departure (and every contract dispute in between), every *This is the year* and every *19-18* chant, every hope, every pain, every thing. All the experiences, in short, of a Red Sox fan. And this, above all else, is why the handshake between Sox fans and Tim Wakefield is so firm, why it is so familiar and so heartfelt; because of time. Because of time, both sides of the handshake understand one another through shared experience, and through those shared experiences Wakefield has become a much different figure for Sox fans than the rock star center fielder or the world-beating slugger. He is seen instead as something much more than these, something closer and more immediate. He has become, quite simply, one of us.

## Wake at Work

Of course, one of the reasons it is easier for Sox fans to imagine Wake as one of our own is because of what he does; or, rather, what he does *not* do, which is anything too awe-inspiring or difficult to comprehend. Most big leaguers do. Throwing a baseball 90 mph; throwing a hard slider to a small spot on the outside corner of the plate; hitting a 90-mph fastball 400 feet in the other direction; hitting a hard slider anywhere; running in and scooping up a ball one-handed, then firing it to first in one smooth motion; the execution of these acts are all beyond even the imagination of most fans. We simply cannot, even in our most delusional bouts of presumption, allow ourselves even the slimmest chance of executing any of these acts, each of which is commonplace on the big league diamond. It is difficult for us then to imagine Pedro Martinez or Johnny Damon (or even Curtis Leskanic and David McCarty) as one of us; their decisively not-like-us talents making it all but impossible. What Wake does, although just as difficult and with just as unique a talent, is less obvious. It seems like something we could learn (or at the very least something we could convince ourselves we could learn).

To start with, he looks like a regular guy; kind of tall, with a trim goatee and the deep, constant tan of a man who works outdoors—the face and look of a farmer, or maybe a fisherman. He steps to the mound with his quick, tiny steps, left-right-left-right, popping the ball in his right hand as he stares at it, examines it. By the time he reaches the rubber, the ball has passed its examination and is ready to be delivered. He takes it in his glove as he looks in to get the sign (not looking *too* hard, we assume) from his personal catcher, Doug Mirabelli. Knuckleball it is. He reaches into his glove, sets his grip, takes one quick step back, and then takes an easy, deliberate stride forward as he holds the ball up above his shoulder with the tips of his fingers, and simply pushes it forward until release. Easy, right?

## *MONSTER* minutiae

Sox fans have learned that it is a different sort of business cheering for a knuckleball pitcher. The basic premise of a knuckleball is unpredictability—the ball floats without rotation toward the plate, and the stationary seams catching slight movements of air cause the ball to jut at random, and often sharp angles, dropping down, sliding over, darting to one side (when a knuckleball is working, it is said to *dance*). This unpredictability is obviously tough on the hitter, so the knuckleballer's job is to make the ball do something completely random, completely its own. This is not what fans are used to cheering for. For instance, when Pedro pitches, Fenway calls out, *Come on, Petey, blow it by him*, or, *Drop the hammer on him*. But with Wake, we rise to our feet, with two outs and two strikes, and shout . . . *Uh, come on, Timmy, really make that ball, um, well, dance, I guess?* It is, in many respects then, quite different with Wake.

The delivery seems simple enough, but not many can mimic its results, which we now see as the ball travels to the plate. Flat and motionless, it floats toward home and the waiting hitter on a pre-scribed path, until at some point it loses its balance and leans too far to the left, sliding awkwardly to port then stopping, suddenly, to set-tle itself. Better now, it sets a new course and just then, just before it reaches the plate, it trips over itself and falls hard, dropping into the dirt as the quiet *whisff*-sound passes just above it. Mirabelli smothers the ball, exchanges it for a new one, and tosses it back to Wake, who then begins the examination again.

Over the previous ten seasons, Sox fans have grown accustomed to this routine, so much so that some (though hopefully not many) may have begun to take its difficulty for granted. This is understand-able, given our familiarity with it. Over the years, we have seen Wake throw knuckleballs as a starter, as a reliever, as a long man, and as a late inning (*uh, Wake, we may have to use you tonight*) emergency reliever. He has done it all, and accepted every role without issue—whatever it takes.

## Lows and Highs

In part, it was this willingness that brought him to the single lowest point in his career and one of the single lowest points in recent Red Sox memory—Game Seven of the 2003 ALCS. In one of the cruelest possible twists to a night that hurt so deeply for so many Sox fans, it was Wakefield, *our boy* Wake, who was on the mound when the final, crushing blow fell on the Sox' 2003 season.

*Not like this*, we said, shaking our heads and muttering, *not Wake; anyone else but Wake.* After it was over, the man himself, like so many of us, was devastated. He feared he would be made the villain by Sox fans, forever reminded of his failure by the incessant boos that would greet him from then on. He should not have feared, for fans responded by embracing him even further, and although he may have asked for our forgiveness, none was required; there was nothing to forgive. (The role of villain in this tragedy had, it turned out, been cast long before Wake took the mound.) He was cheered everywhere he went over the offseason, and given a standing ovation as he accepted an award at the annual Baseball Writers' Association Dinner. The handshake was exchanged again, the past moved past, and life and baseball continued on—as it always does between old friends.

In fact, the only true tragedy fans would later associate with Wakefield in regards to that night was that the ALCS MVP, which was his due after the series, was lost, along with the recognition Wake would have received for having pitched the Sox back into the World Series. It would have been an appropriate, just, and well-deserved honor. As it turned out, this recognition would have to wait a year, and when it finally did arrive, came in a slightly different form. He still pitched the Sox back to the World Series, but this time he did it through one of the most selfless acts of the season. Already down 2-0 in the ALCS and falling down fast and far in Game Three at Fenway, Wake reportedly offered to give up his Game Four start by coming on in relief, which he did in the fourth inning. It was a bad night for everyone associated with the Sox, and for the old Sox it would be no better; he gave up five runs over what must have been three of the most unpleasant innings of his career. By the time he left in the seventh, the grandstands and bleachers were already beginning to thin. It did not seem much at the time—the season was slipping away and whether it was Wake or Lowe who started the next evening hardly appeared to matter much.

But then, the game does not always alert us to the fact that something significant is taking place, and the significance of this moment was only witnessed the following night. After the Sox came back to win Game Four, we immediately realized that because of Wake's sacrifice the Sox would have Pedro and Schilling lined up for Games Five and Six. But Wake was not done pitching, and came on the following night to pitch three arresting innings in the later stages of Game Five—filled with drama, filled with tension—giving up only one hit and holding the Yankees off the board long enough for David Ortiz to do what David Ortiz does. Wake got the win—an appropriate, just, and well-deserved (albeit somewhat belated) honor.

## Our Guy, the Champion

Later on, when the Sox traveled out to St. Louis and completed the four-game sweep that brought them the World Championship, Sox fans of all ages were treated to a number of joyous and deeply satisfying images—the celebration on the field, John Henry accepting the trophy, Johnny Pesky's tears—among them one sight that so many eyes had longed to see for so many years: the sight of Tim Wakefield, drenched in champagne and smiling, cupping the brilliant gold World Series trophy to his side like his firstborn child. Every Sox fan cherished such an image, but particularly the ones who still remember Mike Greenwell's swing and Lee Smith's delivery, and who remember anything at all about Vaughn Eshelman. For these fans, who have watched Tim Wakefield pitch his heart out for the Sox all these years, he has become one of us, one of the boys, one more Sox fan who has been through it all and who understands; and for them, the sight of him holding the trophy was as close as it would ever come to being in their own arms. The sight of him as a champion was the truest proof that we had all come a very long way to get here. Had we Sox fans been there with him, had we come up to him in the clubhouse under a shower of champagne, we would have surely forgone our customary handshake. Championships, like the births of children, are not moments for shaking hands. We would have instead given our boy Wake a hug; a guy-hug, though—a clasped hand and a tucked shoulder and two loud, thick claps on the back (*that'a boy, Wake*)—the kind of hug you give an old friend after a job well done.

**idiot RULE:** *Old friends don't need to shout to get our attention.*

# New Sox

Bronson Arroyo was in the right place, at the right time. The place: Pawtucket; the time: late August, 2003, when the Red Sox bullpen was much in need of reinforcements and when Arroyo just happened to have thrown a perfect game on August 10—and for this we might call him lucky. However it was not luck, but pitching that allowed him to throw the perfect game. (At least it was mostly pitching; there is a certain amount of luck involved in every no-hitter—but, still.) And it was not luck, but a good command of his breaking ball and even better command of his composure, that allowed him to pitch well once he arrived at Fenway, just in time.

# The Fifth (and a Half) Starter

By the time Arroyo appeared in his first game in 2003, the Sox were entangled in an uncomfortable wild card chase with a pair of teams from the West Coast, and were themselves decidedly not in the right place (2nd) at the right time (late August). Sent to the bullpen more as an extra arm than a weapon, his first appearance came at Fenway on August 25, in an extra-innings game against Seattle during which the Sox, not wanting to burn through their already thin bullpen, gave the lanky kid a chance. He pitched well, and earned a save. Then, over the last month of the season, he was given six more appearances, to see how he would do, and again, he pitched well.

Just well enough, as it turns out, to fill the last spot on the Sox play-off roster and be a part of the epic 2003 ALCS. During that series, he pitched in three of the seven games, logged three and a third innings, gave up only one run, and struck out five. His work was noted, and he was invited to spring training in 2004 with the understanding that he would be allowed to compete for the fifth spot in the Sox' starting rotation, but not, ultimately, have a chance to win it.

So Arroyo showed up in Fort Myers, and competed regardless of this understanding, and when the expected fifth starter ended up on the disabled list with a peculiar set of injuries, Arroyo stepped in to fill his place, just in time. This then is how the lanky kid who was brought in as an extra arm to bolster the bullpen ending up standing on the mound at Fenway on April 9, 2004, shortly after the Opening Day ceremonies had concluded, with the ball in his hand. Lucky, huh?

He pitched respectably (6 IP, 4 ER), but not well enough that afternoon, picking up the loss. But he pitched well in relief through the rest of April, and after the intended fifth starter returned and faltered, Arroyo flashed for the first time his D-Lowian penchant for pitching extremely well at the precise moment in the season when he most needed to pitch extremely well. His eight-inning, three-hit shutout in Toronto in mid-May was enough to swing the fifth starter debate in his favor, and he remained in the rotation the rest of the season. And this is how the lanky kid who was brought into the bullpen as an extra arm, who slipped into a playoff spot the previous year when the star acquisition imploded, who slipped into the rotation when another star acquisition self-destructed, and who managed to pitch just well enough all season, ended up coming out of the bullpen in Game Four of the World Series.

## The Thin Man

Both as remarkably tall (6'5") and as remarkably thin (190 lbs) as he appears to be from afar, Arroyo is all joints and levers. His windup, as distinct as any on the staff, only accentuates this fact as he stands completely upright on the mound, right arm at his side and glove held up away from his chest. After receiving the sign from Varitek and nodding (wisely so, as young fifth starters with precarious slots in the rotation do well to not shake off their veteran catchers) he takes one tiny step, almost a slide, back with his left foot and pivots. With his left knee locked, he sweeps his entire leg up in one smooth arc, like a swing on a swingset rocked to its highest point, and points his toes slightly out to third base. He comes to his momentary balance point, waits a beat, then sweeps the leg back down (the swing falling back) and brings the body forward as his hands part and his long right arm pulls back, then out to the side, where it hooks in at about quarter till three. He spins the ball toward the plate as his left leg plants, the body more or less completely upright throughout the entire sequence. A vaguely soothing motion, it reminds us of no other. Once asked how he came up with the unique stiff-leg sweep, Arroyo said it was never really planned, it just felt comfortable that way.

Of course, comfortable or not, the only motion within the motion that ultimately matters is that of the ball once it leaves Arroyo's hand. Everything Arroyo throws has movement—the only difference being to what degree—either the slight last-minute twist of his fastball, or the looping wiffle-ball-like hooks and slices of his more often-used and more effective breaking balls that makes him effective. (Conversely, what makes him *in*effective at times is the simple fact that his pitches lack their normal snap, and instead of diving in and out of the strike zone, they merely spin out over the plate, waiting to be crushed.)

## Whatever

Throwing nothing too hard, nothing too intimidating, Arroyo tends to lull hitters into outs, forcing them to wait back and time up the break and keep their head down and follow the ball all the way to the bat, only to find the ball ducking under their bats as they swing through empty air. And this, too, seems a reflection of the Key West native on the mound, whose laid-back, chilled-out expression never alters from that of an unhurried, unfettered beachcomber—*no worries here* (very un-D-Lowian, this part)—who seems to have strolled into the Red Sox clubhouse in flip-flops, acoustic guitar in hand (he plays, some), and simply grabbed a glove. Told he was starting that night, we imagine Arroyo reacting with the same tranquil expression he holds on the mound. (*Whatever.*)

## *MONSTER* minutiae

Perhaps to break with his understated, unremarkable image, or perhaps inspired by the expressive stylings of his teammates, Bronson Arroyo took to braiding his sandy brown hair into tight, gold-tipped cornrows sometime late in the summer. Sox fans scratched their heads, unsure of what look Arroyo was going for, but certain that it wouldn't last long. But the cornrows stayed—all the way to the mound in Game Four in St. Louis. By that time, the look was no longer something to comment on—it was simply there. (*Whatever.*)

And so both Arroyo and his cornrows were still there once the season and the Series were finally over, and once he had helped make the Red Sox World Champions. For some, his part in the success could be just another sign of Bronson Arroyo being in the right place at the right time. But not for Sox fans; not for those who have paid attention. For while in each and every season there are hundreds of young pitchers (and players, for that matter) who find themselves in the exact right place at the exact right time, not many stay there. Fewer still stay very long.

Arroyo did stay, longer than anyone but perhaps himself ever predicted. While his arriving in Boston was in good part a measure of his pitching well enough to draw attention at the moment attention was ready to be given, his *staying* had little to do with anything other than his ability and, just as significantly, his maturity. Most young pitchers who arrive on the big stages of the big clubs are beaten by the situation long before they are beaten by the hitters, and while Arroyo was no rookie when he came to Fenway, he was given ample opportunity over his first year to feel overwhelmed by the situation. To his credit, he was not, and in fact through most of it appeared distinctly underwhelmed. *It's cool*, he seemed to say, *you know, it's out there*. He was able to ignore both the distractions of the carnival that is the Red Sox Experience and all the expectations that come with it. And in the end, he really was in the right place at the right time, only it was Arroyo himself—who pitched well enough to be called lucky—who had made it so.

**idiot RULE:** *You can find the right place, and you can pick the right time.*

**In a way,** we know Derek Lowe too well. He is too familiar to us, too recognizable. His path and ours run too closely in parallel to allow either much comfort, and because of this, our relationship with him throughout his career (very much like our relationship with the Red Sox throughout their history) has always been something of a struggle. We have pulled him closer to us in triumph, and pushed him farther away in failure than any other player within his generation of Sox, and we have done so with such great frequency and such great conviction because, unlike many of his teammates, to us he is so entirely knowable.

# We and D-Lowe

He is not, like many of his teammates, an enigma. He is not a puzzle and he is not mystery. He is simply D-Lowe. As fans we look at him, and he looks at us, and whatever the circumstances of this look (whether head-shaking disappointment or head-nodding fulfillment), both sides seem to understand one another, in part because there stand no obstacles between the two.

This is not entirely true among many of Lowe's Red Sox teammates, with whom there is at least some buffer of the inexplicable between fan and player. Sox fans adore Jason Varitek, but we tend to do so at a respectful psychological distance. His unwavering strength and almost spartan determination are widely, wholly acclaimed, but there is a mental line at some point between he and us that both sides seem to understand and respect (it is not wise, we remember, to hug the catcher). Similarly with Schilling, whom so many Sox fans speak of with a mixture of admiration and slight, almost paternal, intimidation.

With each, this gap between what we believe we know about each player and what we witness on the field is rather small, but it is there nonetheless. Psychologically, no matter how much we adore or respect a player, this slight gap keeps them (the players) there (on the field), and us (the fans) over here (in the stands). With Derek Lowe, there is simply no such gap. And so when we look at Derek Lowe on the mound we see him too clearly, his emotions too bare and his story too familiar, and feel a slight uneasiness with this familiarity—we know him, and understand him, far too well. When this happens, as it has increasingly throughout Lowe's career with the Red Sox, the lines between him (on the field) and us (in the stands) gradually begin to blur.

## The Mirror on the Mound

We see him there now, on the mound at Fenway, tall no. 32 in all white. Pants to his shoe-tops and tight red sleeves over his long arms, his brown hair shooting from beneath the back of his hat and two days' of stubbly brown growth on his jaw. His face is somewhat long, with a very small (imperceptible to most) scar on the bridge of his nose, and his eyes are wide, active, and at times extraordinarily expressive. At the moment they express focus, concentration, but perhaps, somewhere slightly beneath this focus, a slight but unmistakable pressure (this is not a particularly important midseason, midsummer game for the Sox, but it is, as it always is, a particularly crucial start for Lowe, personally).

He takes the ball on the mound and stretches both arms out high over his head, opening his mouth wide and giving it a stretch at the same time, before bringing glove and ball together in front of him and looking down, to his feet. He sets the back of his heels on the rubber; once set, he looks up and gets the sign. He nods, then takes one tiny step back, body upright and rotating only a degree, pivots on his right foot and brings the left knee straight up (the body upright but hunched slightly at the waist, as if pitching in a very narrow, yet very short phone booth), then breaks as the ball is pulled back and the front leg steps forward one short stride. He plants and holds as the arm swings at a three-quarter angle over the shoulder and delivers, the head and shoulder finally falling off to the left but remaining staunchly upright, watching the ball on its flight.

A sinker, the ball hangs an inch too high a moment too long, and is swatted through the left side of the infield—just wide of Mueller at third and just beyond the reach of Cabrera at short—for a two-out single. Lowe, out in front of the mound, swings his leg out and throws a punch at the air in front of him as we, in the stands, throw up our hands and shake our heads.

He gets the ball back and looks in, his eyes now expressive of the focus building, increasing along with the pressure as we, in the stands, lean forward and focus in, the pressure building. The pitch is a first-ball fastball on the outside corner (a good pitch) but the hitter is disciplined and goes with it, serving it on a low, flat volley over Millar's head and down the right field line. Nixon races over to cut it off and relay it back in for a single. First and third now, still two outs, and we find Lowe, on the field, shuffling back to the mound with his head back, eyes up, shoulders slouched. And we, in the stands, slouch back in our seats and look up, rolling our eyes. He pulls his glove over his mouth and shakes his head as we plant our chin in our hands and shake our head. His eyes grow troubled now, worried as he steps to the mound and we look on with worried, troubled eyes.

The first pitch is a ball, low and inside. The second pitch is a ball inside—a close call. The third pitch bounces in the dirt and is smothered by Varitek, who now calls time and trots out to where Lowe stretches his arms high over his head and paces behind the mound as we, in the stands, stand up in our seats and stretch our arms high above our heads. Varitek finally grabs Lowe's attention as only perhaps he can, and talks his starter down until the nervous, worried pacing calms and the eyes settle. In the stands, we settle in, take a deep breath, and refocus (*come on, D-Lowe*) as on the mound Lowe comes to the set and checks the runners. He steps and throws, a hard sinker in on the hands, swatted away and chopped innocently to second, where Bellhorn scoops and throws to Cabrera at second for the force and the inning, as Lowe charges off the mound and we rise up in the stands, both of us pump our fists and shout a full, triumphant shout.

## CURSE BUSTERS

Varitek and Lowe have always created an intriguing dynamic since arriving in Boston in the now-infamous Heathcliff Slocumb trade with Seattle in 1997. Varitek's strength matched against Lowe's perceived fragility has always made for an interesting contrast, but more interesting has been the way the two seem to be so perfectly suited for each other. Varitek's style of catching and leading appears perfectly suited to grooming and guiding someone of Lowe's complexity, and Lowe's complexity seems to require the guidance of a catcher as determined as Varitek. Is it any wonder that Lowe's most abysmal year (the torturous 2001 season) came during the only season he has consistently gone without Varitek, who missed most of the season due to injury?

We understand the turmoil Lowe has undergone throughout the inning because we underwent the exact same process ourselves and can see it, clearly, reflected in his motions and emotions on the field. Quite simply, Derek Lowe pitches for the Sox like most of us root for the Sox—without restraint, emotionally involved, and reactive to every single pitch of every inning and both physically and vocally expressive of this involvement. In failure, he becomes visibly upset, visibly disturbed, and unabashedly disappointed in the results—just like us. In triumph, he becomes visibly excited, visibly elated, and unabashedly thrilled with the results—again, just like us. He often overreacts to both situations, overdramatizes their significance and overemphasizes either the glory or the gloom of the situation—but then, so do we, far too often than either he or we would care to admit.

We see ourselves then, out there on the mound, when we watch Derek Lowe pitch. And this, of course, is part of the problem. Given the choice, we would rather not see our players (and certainly not our pitchers) reflect the same precarious emotional balance we struggle to hold and far too often lose, in embarrassing fits of melodrama and melancholy, as we live and die with every pitch throughout a nine-inning baseball game. We would just as soon see our pitchers act and react to the game with a calm, rational confidence that we simply cannot be bothered with ourselves.

We want the man on the mound to stand tall with the bases loaded behind him and two outs, and look in at that Hall of Fame slugger, and stare down that 3-0 count as if he could care less, as if this were spring training, as if he resents even the crowd's grumblings because he, and only he, is in complete control of the results of this situation. This would be good (this would be Schilling), and this would be preferable to the pitcher on the mound, staring in and looking every bit as terrified and concerned as we are in the stands, fretting away at our programs and tapping our feet.

But this is Derek Lowe. This is Lowe, who when he fails seems unable to restrain the devastation he feels precisely because he understands, so clearly, the greatness he is capable of. At the same time, this is D-Lowe, who when he succeeds is unable to restrain his joy and elation precisely because he feels, as deeply as every Red Sox fan does, how very close and very real is the constant specter of failure.

## Up and Down

All baseball players understand failure, of course, as it is the concept on which their game is based (the only game not measured in time but in outs; in failures), but some perhaps understand it better than others. Derek Lowe, we may assume, understands it better than most—not because he has failed more or reached greater depths than most, but instead because his many successes, which have brought him up to such great heights, have made the slope down to failure so long and so steep, and because the falls down it have been so complete.

The first of these peaks was reached at the end of the 2000 season, after which Derek Lowe had established himself as one of the elite closers in the game, and he was viewed (much in the same light as the Sox team was viewed) as young and promising and looking forward to bigger seasons and much bigger games.

Then, in 2001, things fell apart. For both. Lowe crashed out as a closer, blowing a number of saves early in the season. He was ultimately replaced by Ugueth Urbina, after which Lowe was relegated to a kind of no-man's land within the Sox bullpen, his utility to the team and his role in its future both very much in question. The Sox themselves crashed out a bit later, but just as spectacularly, blowing a midsummer lead in the division before blowing all sorts of standards for professional baseball conduct, ultimately degenerating into a directionless (and basically managerless) train wreck of dysfunction, on and off the field—the future of the team and franchise very much in question.

By the end, by that unforgettably nightmarish September, both Sox fans and Derek Lowe threw up their hands, out of answers. The ruling on Lowe, concluded on and delivered by the fans, was that he simply was not stable enough to handle the pressure of closing out games—the pressure was too much, and he would never be able to stand up and stand strong when it really mattered the most. It was a damning judgment, made all the more ominous by how closely we recognized this same fault within not only this Red Sox team, but all Red Sox teams. So talented and loose and exuberant in the easy early-summer months, both pitcher and team inevitably seemed to buckle under the pressure of early autumn. Sox fans privately (and at times, not so privately) worried during the dismal October of 2001 how, given this seemingly shared fatal flaw, their troubled pitcher and troubled organization would either ever be saved.

## Down and Back Up Again

Three years later, on a mild Friday night in early October of 2004, we are still worried. We are worried about the Sox—who have waited until the moment we let our worry down (after bringing a 2-0 ALDS lead back to Fenway) to rekindle it with the kind of gothic tragedy we had almost all but forgotten they were capable of, blowing a 6-1 lead in the seventh, capped off by a game-tying grand slam (echoes of 2001). We are worried about Derek Lowe, who we find right where we left him—sitting quietly next to Curtis Leskanic in a kind of no-man's land within the Sox bullpen, his utility to the team and his role in its future very much in question.

He has not been sitting there this entire time, of course, but this hardly matters at the moment, when after a series of late-season melt-downs the Sox as a team and the Sox fans as a people have run out of patience with Lowe and more or less decided to go on without him (there was talk in the media, very serious talk, about leaving him off the playoff roster altogether). Neither starter nor closer, Lowe's role is undefined but understood to be basically that of a last-gasp, emergency option, to be used only when all other options are exhausted. These options—Timlin, Embree, Myers, and Foulke—dwindle through the late innings of Game Three until the Sox are retired in the ninth. The game moves begrudgingly into extra innings, and the Sox bullpen door swings open and no. 32, Derek Lowe, comes sprinting out of the bullpen.

Typically, one of the single most triumphant innings of Derek Lowe's career nearly begins with a minor disaster. His first pitch to Anaheim right fielder Jeff DaVanon is smashed deep into straight-away center, solid and soaring on a low line out toward the wall as Damon races under it, back to the track, and leaps up and back at the last instant to snag the drive and pull it down for the first out. Derek Lowe on the mound, and we in the stands, each let out a long, stabilizing sigh. *Come on, Lowe, easy now.* Lowe steps back to the rubber, sets, and quickly falls behind catcher Jose Molina, 2-0. Then, from way out in the right field grandstands, high up in the crowded, dark seats beneath the roof, comes a gradual, building chant, soft and inaudible at first, then loud and full as it spreads through the crowd to encompass the ballpark—filling it. *Let's-Go, D-Lowe . . . Let's-Go, D-Lowe . . . Let's-Go, D-Lowe.*

It is one of the rare, wonderful moments in a sports venue when the normally ambiguous, normally repetitive crowd chants instead a completely singular message toward one very specific player. In this case, the player is Derek Lowe and the message is simple, unfettered belief. Despite all the troubles in the past, Fenway still holds some remnant of belief in Lowe—that he can overcome the pressure, can become bigger than the moment, and above all, can get the Sox out of this inning and give them a chance to win. We believe in all of this at this moment in much the same way we believe in the Sox as a team—because we want to so desperately—and express both beliefs at the same time in the best way we know how. *Let's-Go, D-Lowe . . . Let's-Go, D-Lowe . . . Let's-Go, D-Lowe.*

Molina walks on five pitches, and the chant dies out before he reaches first. But then Alfredo Amezaga lays a bunt down the third base line, going for a hit, and Mueller charges in hard, scoops with one hand and plants on the run to fire a strike up the line to Mientkiewicz, cutting Amezaga down by a step. And from the same dark corner of the right field grandstand, the same chant rises again. *Lets-Go, D-Lowe . . . Lets-Go, D-Lowe . . . Lets-Go, D-Lowe.*

With one on and two outs now, Lowe steps back up, pounds a sinker in to David Eckstein and forces him to chop a bouncer to short, played effortlessly between hops by Cabrera, who fires across, a step behind the hustling Angel shortstop. First and third now, two outs,

Chone Figgins up. Lowe stretches out his arms over his head and Fenway cheers him on, both he and we understanding the significance of the next out in this game, in this series. Lowe steps and throws, driving a sinker down into the zone and forcing Figgins to chop it up the middle, a soft infield roller behind the mound, which Cabrera charges, scoops, and rips across the diamond in one motion to Mientkiewicz at first—in time—to record the out and end the inning. Fenway roars back to life and showers down applause on Lowe as he hops the first base line, and steps back into the dugout, back to life.

## And Back Down, and Back Up, Again

It is a good story, how a pitcher falls on hard times and then redeems himself later on in a big game, and were this another pitcher on another baseball team, this might be where the story concludes. But this is the Red Sox and this is Derek Lowe, and nothing with either is ever quite so simple. Nor was it during the three years between Lowe's first fall into exile and his ultimate rise out of it. Between the two trips into the bullpen he both fell and rose, rose and tripped and stumbled (and then fell), stood up, dusted himself off, rose to his full height, then took one step and staggered back to a knee, lifted his head, wobbled, and ultimately fell flat once again. And all that in just '02 and '03.

In 2004, Lowe traveled this familiar roller coaster once again— pitched well and then was roughed up a bit, was victimized by poor defense behind him, and then victimized by making bad pitches at the worst possible moments. He struggled, particularly early on in the season, and at one point trade rumors became so thick that the only question was *Who would the Red Sox be able to get for Derek Lowe at this point? Could they get anyone?* It hardly seemed to matter at the time. He simply had to go. The question was not, as it never had been, about talent. Rather, it was determined (by those who determine such things) that Lowe could not mentally handle the strains of pitching in a pressure environment such as Boston.

## *MONSTER* minutiae

Ironic as it may be, one of the last aspects to ever be discussed about Derek Lowe is his tremendous pitching talent. He throws all his pitches with good velocity and with explosive movement, and his sinker is generally acknowledged as one of the best (if not *the* best) in all of baseball. He has, as they say, great stuff, and on his best days he is nearly unhittable—and, on his very best day, he was unhittable, throwing the first no-hitter at Fenway in thirty-seven years on April 27, 2002.

Despite saving 42 games as a Sox closer in 2000 and winning 21 games as a Sox starter in 2002, Derek Lowe was declared mentally unfit to pitch for the Boston Red Sox. He simply could not take the heat, could not take the pressure. He would never, it was said, be able to step up in a big game. To his credit, Lowe rarely took public offense to these claims, as he well might have (most accusations were generally vague, and many were horribly unfair), and he never turned on his teammates who could have easily made life easier for the starter who allowed more unearned runs than any other pitcher in the league. Only once, although memorably, did Lowe take exception to his perceived instability—during one of the particularly rough stretches in early summer 2004. Lowe asked a group of reporters why it was that when another pitcher pitched poorly, it was because he was not "making pitches," while with Lowe it had to be about his mentality? (The answer, of course, is because neither the reporters nor anyone else ever witnessed other starters flail and grimace and shake their heads and otherwise *visibly* melt down on the mound the way Lowe often did.)

Most of the time, though, the criticism was simply hard to dodge. Lowe had pitched poorly, and he admitted as much, but stressed the fact that his struggle was simply to make better pitches rather than straighten out his mental state on the mound. Many nodded, few believed, and most doubted whether he could overcome whatever it was—physical or mental—that kept him from pitching to his fullest potential. More so, and more significantly so, there was the acknowledged worry that Lowe would let the Sox down in some crucial situation—that he could not be trusted to handle the pressure of the really big, really important games the Sox hoped to play in the near future.

And there *would* be very big games, games on which the entire season depended, and in those games, the ball would be trusted in one hand only. Schilling we trusted completely. We often wondered about Pedro, but ultimately believed that his competitive spirit would carry him through. Wake we could rely upon to give us his best effort. But Lowe? To many, he seemed the right man only to orchestrate another colossal Red Sox tragedy, that much we could predict. That much we could see, clearly—Lowe on the mound in a key game, probably against the Yankees, pitching well and then giving up a hit, a walk, an error to load the bases. He would go fuming around the mound, burying his face in the glove, only to return and give up the one really big hit that does in the game, series, and season.

That was how the Red Sox—the historical Red Sox—lost games and wasted seasons; it was part of a past so many fans were so eager to move away from. And so at the end of the 2004 season, Lowe, his underperformance in every big start down the stretch seemingly confirming all previous suspicions, was sent to the bullpen to begin the postseason. The Sox would not plan on giving him the ball to make a postseason start, not this year; this year was different, and this year more stable, more secure arms and minds would be trusted with the ball and the start in the really big games to come.

## The Mirror on the Mound Looks Back

It is only fitting then, later on, that when the moment this Red Sox season seems most in danger of reverting back to the same old tragedy, when it seems that this year really is like all the others, that it should be Derek Lowe—the presence which most embodies this never-ending cycle of rising and falling—who is handed the ball and asked to start Game Four of the ALCS with the Sox trailing the Yankees 3-0. This, of course, is how it should end. It would only be right to have Lowe step in and pitch well, to have him take the Sox deep and then melt down just when the fans believed he could really bring them back. This would be a tragedy worthy of the Red Sox story.

And sure enough, Lowe does pitch well, and he does work hard and battle and keep the Sox close through the middle innings. And sure enough, here it comes—a runner on second with one out in the fifth, Jeter and A-Rod due up—here is how Lowe and the Sox will both come off the rails and crash in one burning heap of intolerable nonsense. But, then, neither come off the rails. Neither crash. We look up to make sure and yes, Lowe comes off the mound and the game is still close. He has, yes, Lowe has pitched a good game, he has pitched a good game in a very big game. Just as he did in the ALDS, Lowe has come in when he was least expected and performed so very unlike what we would expect of him.

He has changed the story, and now as the game grows late and the theatrics of Millar, Roberts, Mueller, and Ortiz give the story another change, the story begins to career in a new direction altogether, something altogether different from what we would expect of the Sox (and certainly of Sox v. Yankees). It is the new Red Sox history, being written over the course of four memorable games on four memorable nights in mid-October 2004, with Derek Lowe right there at the beginning and, later, at the end.

It should not surprise us—we should realize by this point how closely our own story as Red Sox fans fits in with the Derek Lowe story. We should realize that in order for the Sox to finally overcome the Yankees, it would have to come at the hands of someone like Derek Lowe, the unbelievable achieved by the one who was believed in the least—but no matter, it surprises us anyway. It surprises us when Lowe takes the ball once again in Game Seven of the ALCS in Yankee Stadium and pitches sure and solid through its opening innings, then strong and dominant through its middle third. But it surprises us even more how he does this, how calm and how confident he seems, completely in control of himself and the moment. And the reason it should not surprise us, at this point, is because we too, at this point, feel something of this confidence. This really is the year, this is how it is going to happen, just like this—and every out only strengthens this confidence (his and ours). It is inarguably the single biggest start of Derek Lowe's career in arguably the single biggest game in Red Sox history, the exact moment so many doubted he could ever triumph in just as so many doubted the Red Sox, as a team, could triumph in this exact moment. Both proved all doubters wrong, both rewarded all believers. Both exorcised their darkest, most haunting demons on the very same night on the very same field—just as one sensed, by this point, it had to be.

## You, Me, and D-Lowe

It has always been one of the more intriguing questions among Red Sox fans, as we sat around on dark New England winter nights or under the drizzly, damp Fenway concourses during an endless rain delay—*Who,* we asked each other, *will be the hero*? The rest of the sentence (the, *of what*) is left off because it is understood—when we ask this, we are allowing ourselves to wonder who will be our golden World Series hero. For a very long time, the easy and obvious answer was Pedro. Then, gradually, Manny. Later on, with such a track record to support him, Ortiz was the only real candidate. Then, coming into the 2004 season, the case was made for Curt Schilling. These arguments went back and forth, as they often do, and a spare wild card was thrown in (Damon, perhaps) without ever hitting on the one true answer.

Looking back now, we should have known better. Looking back, we can see that within this generation of Red Sox players, there has been only one figure who has so closely paralleled the Sox' path over the previous eight seasons, whose own personal trials and triumphs have so mimicked the trials and triumphs of the team as a whole; only one figure whose every failure has echoed a team failure, and whose every redemption has reflected a team redemption, every step of the way.

The 2004 season proved no different—a maddening, frustrating series of false starts and abrupt reversals for both Lowe and the Sox—and so why should we ever have expected anything different in the 2004 playoffs? This, of course, was how it seemingly had to be. If the Red Sox were to ever overcome their sad history of shocking, sudden reversals, such a reversal would have to be denied by the one man who stood as living proof of so many similar turns of fortune. So they did, and so there he was—Derek Lowe, the winner of the deciding game in the 2004 ALDS. And if the Red Sox were to ever finally cast off the legions of painful memories and dark, personal demons tied up in their rivalry with the Yankees, the final blow would have to be thrown by the man who stood as living proof that so many personal demons could be cast off. So they did, and so there he was—Derek Lowe, the winner of the deciding game in the 2004 ALCS. And, finally, if the Red Sox were ever to change their history of falling desperately short in their championship hopes, of keeping their fans faithful to the verge of losing that faith, the only possible man to bring about such a change would be the one figure in whom faith and belief were lost and regained so many times. So they did, and so there he is—Derek Lowe, the winner of the deciding game in the 2004 World Series.

In the end, the story of Derek Lowe, through all of his struggles, became something of the Red Sox story incarnate. He is not, perhaps, who we fans would have chosen for such a title. We would have certainly preferred the Red Sox story—and our personal Red Sox story—to look much more like Curt Schilling, who comes in and says he is going to do something and then does it. End of story. Or, we might not have minded if our story looked more like Manny, playing in the dugout and laughing on the basepaths, carefree and easy, continuing to move and continuing to make his own destination. That would not have been so bad, after all. Our worry, however—our greatest fear, even—was that the Red Sox story did in fact look very much like Derek Lowe, and would very closely follow along his path.

This is how we watched both him and the Red Sox together, publicly stating they were as talented and capable as we believed them to be, while secretly harboring deeply held fears that they would, despite this talent, only break our hearts in the end. So many of us carried this odd, uncomfortable mixture of baseball confidence and personal doubt with us as we followed the Sox over the past eight years of their resurgence; and this too was how we followed the eight-year career of Derek Lowe.

The two experiences were one and the same, and this, above all else, is why Derek Lowe is too familiar to us, is too much with us, and why we sometimes feel as if we know him far too well. Our greatest hope was that the Red Sox would prove our fears wrong, would not in fact break our hearts in the end, but be every bit as good as we believed they could be. In the end they—the Sox and Lowe—were this good, every bit as good as we imagined.

The only question we still have yet to answer is how they did it. We still, even now, wonder how Lowe overcame so much doubt and so much negativity to pitch so brilliantly in Game Seven, just as we still wonder how the Sox as a team overcame such tremendous odds to make Game Seven possible. We may never know how Lowe was able to step up and perform like a champion in Game Four of the World Series, just as we may never know how the Sox, after so many reversals throughout their history and season, were able to push on and sweep the Cardinals in such a dominant fashion—so becoming of a true champion.

But even this wonder, this amazement, is familiar to us as fans. None of us, it seems, know how we made it through either. We may never know exactly how we put up with all the heartbreak, how we dealt with all the disappointment, or how we were able to put such troubles behind us and come back again each year renewed, re-energized, and full of hope. It seems a minor miracle to us now, and it is not our place to question miracles (minor though they may be).

The word *somehow* will have to do. Somehow we made it, some-how we came back each year and somehow we kept showing up; somehow we got over '78 and '86 and '03, and somehow found a way to believe in '79 and '87 and '04; and somehow we hung on, even down 3-0, and somehow we believed they would find a way, and somehow, they did.

They did it, somehow, the Red Sox won the World Series and somehow we were there to watch and listen, to jump and shout and maybe even cry a bit toward the end when we looked around and saw everyone there, everyone who had made the trip with us—

Wake and Nixon and your Uncle Marty on the Cape, Pedro and Manny and your mom up in New Hampshire, Ortiz and Millar, your cousin Jenn and your brother Sean, Theo and John Henry and the kid you used to pretend was Fisk when you pretended to be Luis Tiant, your roommate from college and Tek, your best friend Bill who moved away and your next best friend Sarah who stayed home, your other brother Brian, and Billy Mueller and your dad way out in western Mass. *Somehow*, we were all there in the end. All of us. And you. And even me and D-Lowe, too.

**idiot RULE:** *Even if you only have one chance left, you still have a chance.*

# Chapter 13

# The Bullpen

## The Accidental Closer

**The bullpen door swings open** at the end of the eighth, the crowd in the bleachers leaning forward over their scorecards in anticipation as a pair of deep base notes sound from the loudspeakers at Fenway, followed by the low bellowing voice of Glen Danzig calling out, warning us all, *Mother, tell your children not to walk my way*. It is a menacing bit of advice and although its appearance here at Fenway is hardly intended to be humorous (quite the opposite), there is an unmistakable touch of comic irony at work as we watch a relatively short, squat, and remarkably unmenacing pitcher jog out across the outfield grass beneath the warning.

## First Impressions

Looking around us to see if anyone else has noticed the gap between the overtly intimidating sounds we hear and the obviously unintimidating sight we see, we notice a few shared smiles rippling out among the Fenway bleachers. (*It is kind of funny, in a way.*) After all, the last time we saw Keith Foulke before he signed as a free agent in December of 2003, he was blowing Oakland's series-clinching lead in Game Four of the ALDS, right here at Fenway. This lasting image of failure in a season-deciding situation led some of us to pose the question, "Do you really want Keith Foulke on the mound with the World Series on the line?"

But this is an early summer scene, taken from a relaxed moment in April—the ballpark still stretching out its new additions, the bars still draped with wide *Welcome Back Sox Fans* banners—and so we Sox fans can perhaps be forgiven our misreading of (and our failure to see the intimidation within) our brand-new closer. We at Fenway take ourselves to be an educated, sophisticated lot, understanding the newest methods of evaluating talent, and far beyond such base, archaic means of sizing up a player simply by his appearance. But then, we too are human, and we too can be deceived.

So then, Keith, for all of us who raised a skeptical eyebrow and privately questioned the appropriateness of your musical selection, we would now like to apologize. We're sorry—we simply didn't know.

## But...

In our defense, we may cite the fact that we have grown accustomed to certain images of what a closer should and should not look like and, much more importantly, how a closer should and should not pitch. First and foremost, we expect our closers to be intimidating, both in look and in action. After all, this is the man whose job is so often described as "coming in to *slam the door shut.*"

We often think of the stereotypical closer commanding a physically intimidating presence, usually taking one of two forms, either: 1) that of the hard-charging Wild Bull, huffing-and-puffing his way to the mound, working himself into a fury as he paces nervously around the mound, eventually staring in at the hitter with palpable menace. The Wild Bull is usually a big guy who throws hard, sometimes hazardously near the hitter (for examples of this type, see: Percival, Troy; or, less recently but more ideally: Rocker, John). Or, 2) the Icy Stoic, standing completely still on the mound and staring in with an unflinching glare that says to the hitter, *We both know I am not the one who should be nervous in this situation* (for examples of the Icy Stoic, look absolutely no further than: Rivera, Mariano).

Then of course there is the actual pitching itself. There are a number of variations in style here as well, from the arsenal of pitches used by Eric Gagne to the singularly effective, single-bullet of Mariano Rivera's cutter. But by far the most popular and most imposing weapon we have come to expect from our closers is the single most basic and single most intimidating pitch in all of baseball—the fastball. Specifically the hard fastball, preferably delivered somewhere around 95 to 98 miles per hour, thrown without variance or mercy. While other pitchers can rely on deception—changing speeds, mixing pitches, varying locations—what most fans expect from their closer is not so much art as firepower. With the game (or the season) on the line, our casual, early-inning thoughts of control and elegance and craft are briskly shoved aside as we narrow our focus to a simpler desire—to see our guy overpower their guy, and to do so rather quickly.

The fan's idealized image of the closer, then, would be that of a very large, very unpleasant figure bolting from the bullpen door (breaking down the bullpen door, ideally) and charging to the mound to glare in at the hitter and (as we gather our scorecards and jackets and cameras) throw nine consecutive 99-mph fastballs about knee-high on the inside back of the plate. Ideally then, opposing hitters would fear God and, only slightly less so, our closer.

## *This* Is Our Closer?

Standing at exactly six feet tall, and weighing in at around 210 lbs, Foulke cuts a stout, slightly bottom-heavy figure on the mound, his legs and haunches the solid base on which his midsection is set; but his most obvious (and most telling) proportions come in the size of his thick forearms, particularly the meaty heft of his Popeye-esque right arm.

Looking at us from under the bill of his hat we see that he has a soft, round face, with unassuming eyes and a wide, flat smile;

altogether a disarming, vaguely Canadian face, which had we not been introduced to through baseball, we might have pegged for that of a harmless, vaguely Canadian mailman.

No matter. We know from experience (and from Billy Wagner) that a diminutive figure and an affable face can still be daunting, as long as it all gets behind a blazing fastball or a devastating slider. So we give this benefit to our new closer as he steps to the mound. Left shoulder plateward, the ball hangs behind his right thigh at the end of his beefy right forearm. He gives his right arm a quick shake before he looks in and gets the sign, then brings both glove and ball together away from his body as his bottom half settles into a slight crouch.

At this moment we notice two details at once: the first a large embroidered flag on the base of his glove—red, white, and blue, for his Texas home—and the second the fact that he is sweating. Sweating quite a bit, actually. His brow, cheeks, chin, and upper lip are all damp with tiny beads of perspiration, as is his exposed right forearm (thus the quick shake prior to coming set). Over the course of the season, Sox fans will become familiar with a reflex habit connected to this sweating—Foulke wiping off his upper lip with the collar of his jersey. (Gone then, with all this sweat, is the cool stoic approach of a typical closer.)

Still crouched and still holding glove and ball away from his body, Foulke gives a slow, craning glance back, chin to left shoulder, at a runner leading off first, then immediately pushes off, separating hand from glove as he stretches his right arm back and holds the ball away, facing the centerfield bleachers, and pushes off with his back leg to deliver the pitch—a change-up, on the corner, clocking in at around 78 mph. (Gone then, with the pitch that is the very essence of deception, is the overpowering approach.)

And so at first glance we are not much impressed with the *look* of our new closer, and on second glance we are not much more impressed with the *style* of his pitching. Sitting in the Fenway bleachers during the first, chilly homestand, we allow ourselves a wry smile, a skeptical raise of the eyebrow, and a few slightly incredulous remarks as No. 29 jogs out across the outfield grass. But this is our own shortcoming, and not his.

## The Change-Up

Although many fans questioned his makeup and his ability, and even more questioned his reliability in crucial, season-defining moments, in the end we learned that he had fooled us all. Along the way he fooled a great many others, of course, not the least of whom were the majority of American League hitters he faced, too. How exactly he managed this is still something of a mystery (to us and to them, surely), but a hint of it can be found in the nature of his signature pitch—the aforementioned change-up—and how it uses the hitter's natural instincts against him. Like the fans surrounding him, the hitter who steps to the plate in the crucial late innings of a close game can feel the atmosphere in the ballpark tighten as he faces the closer. He knows what is on the line (be it season, series, or game), and knows what is expected of him, and knows that in a short time he will be asked to give account of how he either did or did not meet those expectations. The grip clenches a bit tighter, the feet dig in a bit deeper, the breathing comes a bit quicker as the closer readies himself.

Foulke uses his change-up to turn this very same focus against the hitter. Hitters hope their eyes-mind-hands reflexes are disciplined enough to sit back and *wait, wait, wait* on the change-up. This is difficult enough during any at-bat, but becomes much more challenging in the late innings when the game is on the line and the crowd is on its feet and one late reaction to a fastball could mean a night of second-guessing and disappointment. The hitter tells himself to *be patient, stay back, relax, wait, wait, wait,* but when the pitch comes the eyes-mind-hands reflex takes over and triggers the swing and pivots the hips and drops the hands and throws the bat out ahead of the falling change-up, which now sits in the catcher's mitt for strike three. This is how the change-up is designed to work, and Foulke's ability to throw it so well, so consistently, and so relentlessly is one of the keys to his success.

## MONSTER minutiae

Because the change-up is a pitch designed to work in tandem with another pitch, it is not often advisable to throw it over and over to the same hitter (the point being if it is not "changing up" off anything, then it becomes simply a very slow, very hittable pitch). But Foulke will throw three, four, or sometimes five change-ups in a row to the same hitter. And you can see the hitter thinking, *No way, no way he throws me another change-up here.* They look for the fastball, then shake their heads after missing the change-up. *No way.*

But there is another, slightly less obvious but perhaps just as significant factor at work behind Keith Foulke's success, and it is based on the same reflex assumptions we as fans made upon first assessing our new, slightly unimpressive looking closer. Because the hitter sees the same Keith Foulke as we do. He sees the stout frame, the soft, disarming face, the same 90 mph fastball, the same change-up, the same lack of hard breaking stuff. He sees all this and, like us, he is not much intimidated. And so he thinks: *I can hit this guy.* We find evidence of this misguided assumption in the approach certain hitters have taken to Foulke throughout his career, but one instance in particular stands out from one of the very first tight, critical moments of the Sox' playoff run. In the bottom of the ninth of the ALDS finale at Fenway, with the game tied and the bases loaded, Troy Glaus stepped up to face Foulke in the middle of a frenetic, nerve-fraying atmosphere at Fenway (the game had been a trying one already), needing only a bloop single to push across the go-ahead run. The first pitch he saw from Foulke was, predictably enough, a change-up that Glaus swung at so hard but so very early. A thread of *wow*s ran beneath the cheers and applause for strike one.

Glaus, apparently, was not thinking bloop single. We may venture a guess that it was somewhere along the lines of, *you and I both know that you can't throw anything past me, and you and I both know that you won't walk me here, so I'm going to make sure that if I make contact this game is over.* (Or something like that.) Glaus is a justifiably confident, aggressive hitter, and no doubt respects Foulke as a professional, but would he have taken the same sky-cleaving hack at Billy Wagner's 99-mph fastball, or at Mariano Rivera's bat-breaking cutter? Would he not have looked to just make contact, bloop a single over second base, and give his team the lead? Impossible to say, but evidence suggests that he, like so many others, looked out at the mound and felt he could handle whatever the sweaty closer facing him could deliver. Glaus looked out and was unimpressed, unafraid, and unintimidated—and because of this was ultimately, like all the rest of us, fooled.

## CURSE BUSTERS

The very reason Keith Foulke was brought to Boston was to correct the Red Sox' now-infamous 2003 closer-by-committee philosophy, which declared that there was no such thing as a closer at all—that the final three outs of a game are no different in tone, and no more difficult to record, than any others. The problem with this system, however, is that pitchers have eyes, and when those eyes see a scoreboard indicating a close game in the ninth inning, the brain behind those eyes tells a whole bunch of nerve endings that making a mistake now is very different from making a mistake in the fourth. Thus, the Sox and their fans learned the hard way during the 2003 season that not every inning is the same, not every out is the same, and certain pitchers are better suited to record certain outs in certain innings. The difference in 2004 was simply using our toughest pitcher, Foulke, to come in and record the tough, final outs.

At the root of this deception is the very simple, very obvious lesson that most of us learn in grade school but quickly forget: Things are not always as they appear to be. Keith Foulke may not look like we expect a closer to look, and he may not even pitch like we expect a closer to pitch, but this hardly means that he does not possess all of the crucial traits that go into the makeup of a dominating closer.

## Lights Out

What specifically makes Keith Foulke the right pitcher to record those last, tough outs is something that cannot be seen but can be felt and understood, and therefore it can be appreciated. And at no point was Foulke's worth more deeply felt, or more deeply appreciated than during Game Four of the ALCS—when Foulke's $2^2/_3$ hitless innings provided the eight crucial outs that allowed for Ortiz's eventual game-winning home run, which in turn allowed for the Sox historic comeback, which in turn allowed for the red banner that will soon hang outside of Fenway.

It was during those innings, and in the innings that followed in Games Five, Six, and Seven that Red Sox fans understood what Troy Glaus had learned a week earlier: that Keith Foulke is a fighter, that he competes every single pitch of every single at-bat, and that he will never give in to a hitter or succumb to the moment. He is a fearless competitor, and this, more than any other trait—more than the blinking fastball or the devastating slider—is the one quality a closer cannot do without. Keith Foulke has this and little else other than a pretty good change-up, but in the end it is all he ever needed—to be a great closer, to close great games, and to close out a championship.

The ALCS taught us this lesson, and so when the bullpen door swings open in Game One of the World Series and a pair of deep base notes sound from the loudspeakers at Fenway, followed by the low bellowing voice of Glen Danzig calling out, and No. 29 tosses a ball into the bleachers and jogs out onto the outfield grass, it all makes sense—the song, the figure, the confidence we feel as we watch him step to the mound, it all seems to work together. The deep, appreciative roar that rises throughout Fenway at this moment (*sorry, Keith, now we know*) is filled with this understanding. It hardly matters that the situation he now enters into—the bases loaded in a tie game, one out, and Scott Rolen at the plate—should fill us not with understanding but with dread.

We have overcome—well, *almost* overcome—our skepticism by now, and it comes as no surprise to us when Foulke forces Rolen to pop weakly over the infield, and it comes as even less of a surprise when, moments later, he strikes out Jim Edmonds to end the inning and the threat. An inning later he slams the door, one-two-three, to end the game; then does the same the following night to end Game Two; and is once again on the mound to record the last three outs of Game Three.

And so it is taken for granted when the following night, it is Keith Foulke who takes the ball and steps to the mound in Game Four with the World Series Championship three outs away. It only seems right, but we do not have to remember too far in the past to know that this was not always the case, to recall that there was a point when many doubted whether this rather short, rather unremarkable-looking man from South Dakota—whose favorite sport is still hockey—was the right man to take the ball in such a history-making situation. In the end he was the right man, and he did bring the Sox to this situation, and it only makes sense that moments later, when Edgar Renteria chops a change-up into the dirt, that the ball should hop back to where it began, in Keith Foulke's glove. And as he squeezes it and takes two careful steps toward first and lobs it softly to Mientkiewicz for the final out, it only makes sense that this unlikely closer should find himself at the center of this most unlikely celebration.

The full-page photo in the *Globe* the following Sunday—after the celebratory champagne had been wiped away in the St. Louis clubhouse and after the confetti had been swept up from the Boston streets—showed Doug Mientkiewicz in the background, slightly blurry, arms skyward and feet off the ground as he leaps in celebration. In the upper-right hand corner is the date (10.27.04), and below it the time (11:40 pm), and below it the location (St. Louis), and below that Joe Castiglione's call of the final play. And just below the last line, underneath the large bold words *Can you believe it?* is the foreground image of Keith Foulke, pumping his fist and turning in midair toward his on-rushing catcher. It is the one image and one moment that will remain forever fixed in the minds of every living Red Sox fan, for as long as any images remain with them. There, right in the middle of that indelible image, is Keith Foulke, reminding us of the rhetorical question his critics in Boston once used against him, when they looked skeptically over both him and his change-up and asked, "Do you really want Keith Foulke on the mound with the World Series on the line?" Our answer, now if not then, is yes.

We wouldn't have it any other way.

**idiot RULE:** *Look for the fastball, but always be ready for the change-up.*

# Timlin & Embree, Together Again

In the two seasons Mike Timlin and Alan Embree have spent together in the Red Sox bullpen, their names have been mentioned independently of one another, either among fans or within the Boston media, approximately five times. Possibly six, but no more. At all other times, the two have been connected in both thought and in conversation as Timlin & Embree, and this is how they are spoken of, both by fans and media: *Yeah, he used Timlin & Embree last night,* or, *Timlin & Embree can still go tonight,* or, *Look, we get two out of Timlin & Embree and we're solid.* And so on.

## The Trusted Two

In part, this is due to consistency and familiarity—the two middle relievers have, over the past two seasons, been the only familiar, constant elements in an otherwise fluctuating bullpen. They have also appeared in more games, both individually and more often in tandem, over that same period than any other Sox pitcher (*ehem*, pitch-ers). But more than this, Timlin & Embree have become a single, unified quantity in the minds of Red Sox followers for the very basic and yet important fact that both men are trusted, and that a great deal of trust is placed in them as a pair.

The word *trust* tends to come up quite a bit when fans talk of middle relief, and for good reason. We set high standards for the starter—to pitch well and to win games. Likewise we set high standards for the closer as well—to never allow a single run and to save the game in the end. Middle relief, however, seems to be an area where, although just as crucial, the expectations are reduced to one very simple request: *Look, we're not asking for anything spectacular here. Just get the ball from the starter to the closer. That's all.*

But then *that* adds up to a great deal in the course of a game and a season, and because the need for a middle reliever arises almost nightly (if things are going well), and because consistency is such a rarely attained quality in relief pitching, the essential element between fan and middle reliever is this business of trust. Without it, all names and all arms are suspect.

## MONSTER minutiae

Bullpen life is nearly always nomadic, and a good relief pitcher does well not to write down the names and phone numbers of his bullpenmates in ink. And the Sox bullpen in 2003–04 had an especially busy door. In just two seasons, Timlin & Embree have seen a total of 32 faces come and go. Needless to say, during that time, they were the only constants.

One of the more popular refrains among fans discussing bullpen matters is the simple, *I just don't trust him*, or the rhetorical, *Do you trust him with a one-run lead?* The answer, if the question is even being asked, is *no*. The pitcher is then marked as suspect in the minds of the fans, and usually for good. Distrust is the scarlet letter among relievers, and once received, it becomes nearly impossible to remove. And because trust itself is more easily lost than gained, the majority of middle relievers are looked upon by the fans with some degree of skepticism. Even when a formerly disastrous reliever turns things around a bit, maybe pitches well for a few outings, the stain of his failures is always visible to the fans, and trust becomes extremely difficult to regain in its presence (see: Mendoza, Ramiro).

That's why Timlin & Embree have gained such solid ground with both fans and media. The sound of their names together is a comfort blanket, the solid, affirming answer to any number of troubling questions. What if Schilling can only go six? *No worries, Timlin & Embree.* What if Foulke can't go two again tonight? *We've still got Timlin & Embree.* What if the starter comes out early in a tie game? *Timlin & Embree.* What if the starter loses his control in the middle of the fifth? *Timlin & Embree.* What if our car breaks down in the middle of the Pike on the drive home? *Timlin & Embree.* Feel better? Sure we do.

# The Second Half

Throughout the past two seasons, Sox fans have grown accustomed to looking into the bullpen for one sight: Timlin & Embree. It may come as some surprise to those fans at Fenway who only know of the bullpen through conversation that Timlin & Embree are actually a pair of players. Their names are Mike Timlin and Alan Embree, and they are in fact two completely separate men.

We can see this clearly now, with Embree taking the mound in Game Two of the World Series and Timlin seated in the bullpen. For the record, Alan Embree is the shorter (6'2"), slimmer (190 lbs) of the two, is No. 43 in your program, and also, quite significantly, throws with his left hand rather than his right. He has come into this game in prime Timlin & Embree time, the seventh, following six soon-to-be legendary innings from starter Curt Schilling, and would very much like to avoid being the man to blow the Sox lead and simultaneously spoil said legendary performance. He strikes out the first man he faces, and now steps back to the mound to face Cardinals catcher Mike Matheny.

Without sleeves and with his white pants stretching to the tops of his cleats, Embree holds an upright, shoulders-back posture as he steps to the rubber, his right shoulder aimed directly at home. His stiff, brand-new blue hat sits squarely on his head, perched an inch above his ears, with his sandy brown goatee trim; all making for an impressively up-and-down figure, everything to spec. In fact, the only irregularity in this almost militarily precise image is the rather large knob stretching out from the right cheek. This small seismic event on Embree's face represents his chaw, and over the course of the season this deformation has at times become so exaggerated, the cheek so stretched, the jaw so overmatched, that it has been almost painful to watch. But by October, we have come to understand this as simply part of what makes him Alan Embree.

## *MONSTER* minutiae

Occasionally, even the separation of their names has caused trouble, as among the Fenway bleachers the two have occasionally been jokingly referred to by fans as either Mike Emlin, or Alan Timbree.

Similarly, we have come to watch the seismic movements of this knob, and noticed that at times, it gives slight, subtle indications of what we might expect from the performance. When the cheek is overstuffed—when Embree has sat in the bullpen and crammed more and more chaw into every last crevice of his jaw, and when he steps to the mound and works said mass relentlessly as he nervously paces the mound—it does not bode well for the Sox or their slim lead. However, when the mountain is but a considerable hill, when it is impressive but not sublimely so, and when it is controlled in one area of one side of the jaw, as it is this night, then we expect good things from our hard-throwing lefty.

Embree stands feet-together on the rubber, getting the sign from Varitek and staring straight out to an unoccupied first base. He lifts both ball and glove high (inhale) and connects both away from his body, then slowly brings both down (exhale) as he drops them to his hips and brings his eyes down to the ground just left of the mound— and pauses. Then, still looking down, he brings his front leg up with ball and glove to a balance point, holds a beat, and breaks his hands as he pushes forward and at the very last instant looks quickly to home as he brings his stiff left arm sweeping down across his body. The ball darts in on Matheny's hands as he swats helplessly—strike three. The pitch was a fastball, a sharp flat, precise line, both direct and effective; and this, then, is who Alan Embree is and what Alan Embree does. Like all pitchers, he has not always done this effectively, but over the past two seasons he has done so with enough consistency and reliability to be trusted with a lead in the seventh inning of Game Two of the World Series.

## . . . And the First Half

This lead still needs protecting an inning later when Embree leaves and gives way to Timlin. The taller (6'4"), broader (210 lbs) of the two, and No. 50 in your program, Mike Timlin is the righty of the righty-lefty combination. With his red socks pulled knee high and red sleeves stretching out of his baggier white uniform, Timlin the slightly rougher, slightly less precise of the two—both in appearance and performance. His hat is broken in and crooked, dusted with chalk, and creased in two places across the bill. We see only a small, almost imperceptible bump on the right side of his jaw (which we suspect might be larger had Embree not claimed the bullpen's chaw rations).

Timlin shifts and shrugs as he takes the ball and circles the mound. He steps to the rubber and faces Larry Walker with his shoulders pointed at a slight angle toward first. His face, tough and weathered and somehow expressive of his considerable experience in the league, is turned directly in toward Varitek, from whom he receives the sign and comes set.

## CURSE BUSTERS

When Timlin first came to the Red Sox, he was entangled in the ill-fated Bullpen by Committee experiment and was booed during the introductions at his Fenway debut, along with the rest of his bullpenmates. It was an embarrassing moment for fans and a troubling first impression for hopeful new players. Timlin, however, rose above the moment. He understood why fans booed. It was okay. When they pitched better, the fans would cheer. That's how the game works. At the time, he seemed to show astounding restraint, and yet that became the kind of mature, adult, and above-all professional manner we came to expect from Timlin.

It is a good face, an honest face, the kind of face you can trust. He comes set, and when he delivers, there is nothing peculiar about the motion, nothing fussy or extravagant—no high leg kick or look to the air, no odd arm angle or distinctive follow-through—he simply steps and throws. He lifts the front foot, keeps the front shoulder in, pushes off, drives the shoulder down, snaps the arm through and delivers, and the pitch cuts in and breaks down at the last instant. Walker swings and chops it into the ground, back to Timlin, who fields it and throws to first for the out.

This fastball is one of a variety of pitches Timlin throws, at a variety of speeds and in a variety of situations; and this, then, is who Mike Timlin is and this is what Mike Timlin does. Because while Timlin mixes in a breaking ball now and again, and will adjust location relative to the hitter, Embree's style is much more direct. He throws a hard fastball, and he throws it often. Most of the time he throws it by hitters; other times he does not. Timlin, relative to Embree, works with a range of pitches and relies on mixing them up, with no one pitch (the hard sinker is his best, but is not dominating enough to stand alone) predominant. A veteran pitcher, an old Texan with an old broken-down hat, when Timlin steps to the mound he does not so much throw as work, and work hard; and this, in New England, is as good a way as any to earn a well-deserved measure of trust.

## Together Again

And so Timlin & Embree are our way of getting from six to nine, of getting from Schilling to Foulke. Their job is not often celebrated, as there is very little glory involved for the middle relievers who act as the steady, reliable bridge between a memorable, exciting start and a memorable, thrilling finish. But the men in the middle do not seem to have come for acclaim so much as they have come to work, and to do a job. And by doing it consistently and reliably, they have earned something from the fans that is both more difficult to gain and less easy to keep—they have gained our trust.

Far too often, the glance down into the bullpen during the late innings has caused the opposite reaction—skepticism and doubt—and far too often, this doubt has been justified by the performance that later comes from within said bullpen. But Sox fans, for whom nothing may cause more nervous misgivings than a slim Sox lead, have had one image that has the power to calm all doubts—one sight that causes if not peace, at least a reserved confidence, an emotion very close to optimism.

And this is the sight one takes in when the starter exits to the rousing ovation of Fenway, tips his cap and steps into the dugout, and we in the bleachers stand and crane out to look down into the bullpen, and there we see them—big No. 50 on the right, slim No. 43 on the left, Timlin & Embree, side by side on the bullpen mound, throwing in tandem. We can even hear the snapping *pop-pop* of two catchers' mitts at the other end. We nod, to them, to ourselves, and to each other. *All right, good.* We could use a few more runs here, certainly; we would like to have capitalized on that bases-loaded situation in the second, and brought in that runner from third in the fifth; we would like to have back that 3-2 pitch in the first, and would have loved to have turned that double play in the third.

But still, things are all right, and with one more steady glance down to the bullpen we lean back in our seats. We're good—it is a warm, comfortable summer night at Fenway, the Sox have the lead, and there, warming up in the bullpen, are Timlin & Embree, together again.

## idiot RULE: *It takes two.*

# Theology

**In the cool gray hours** leading up to Game Four of the 2004 ALCS, with the Red Sox trailing the Yankees 3-0 and within one loss of a devastating, season-ending sweep, Sox General Manager Theo Epstein sits behind a microphone facing both the national and international baseball press corps, and answers questions. He is clean-shaven, with a calm, flat mouth and dark, steady eyes. His brown hair is cropped low and close. He is thirty years old. And he is not smiling.

The questions come quick and hurried from each reporter, the urgency of the moment and the magnitude of its possibilities crackling just beneath the surface of each question. Epstein listens with a slight tilt of the head but otherwise holds the stoic gravity of his expression firm. He answers each question with an even, measured diction, utterly calm and unfailingly composed—a dour businessman discussing a dour business. A few of the questions he fields concern present issues, the present game and the present series; and a few deal with the past, with the historical precedents of the present situation and its historical outcome. But most of the questions are concerned, instead, with the future. How will the Red Sox in general and Epstein in particular deal with the inevitable loss to the Yankees? How will they approach their now-imminent offseason? Will the loss to the Yankees, in perhaps humiliating circumstances, change how Epstein and the organization approach their many high-profile free agents? How, in the end, will they recover from this tragedy?

Epstein listens to each question with the same slight tilt of the head and low, peering-back gaze, then carefully answers each with the same even, measured diction as he tells the room, repeatedly, that these are questions for another day. The future can wait. In the meantime, he points out, his club is still only four games away from the World Series—a factually true statement that is still somewhat misleading (*Yes, Theo, but of course, these are not just* any *four games*). It is a position that is not easily reached and should not be easily dismissed; not as long as there is still baseball to be played. His focus, he says, is on the game the Red Sox are preparing to play in a few hours, and nothing more. Epstein sits up straight behind the microphone, looks out with steady eyes over the pressroom full of reporters, and repeats this statement. At the present moment, he stresses repeatedly, the future is not his concern.

# A Man for the Future

It is an odd, uncomfortable stance for Epstein to take, given his professional obligation and personal commitment to concern himself with little else *other* than the future of the Boston Red Sox. But the circumstances of the moment have forced this stance upon him, as the events of the past five days have made both his and the Red Sox' future imminently present. Yet, though his mind may (and perhaps must) linger on the upcoming months and even years ahead of the Red Sox organization, his words must at this moment pay the appropriate respect to the current club—the club he has assembled and who may be preparing to play their last game together.

It is not, by any means, a situation in which Epstein should be comfortable. His position does not require him to prepare for such moments, and his substantial intellect and rigorous management skills are not calibrated to focus as narrowly as one, single baseball game. It is, quite simply, not his job. Instead, his job is the future—specifically, the future success of the Boston Red Sox Baseball Club. This was the job he was handed in November of 2002, when at twenty-eight years and eleven months, he became the youngest general manager in baseball history. The future of the Red Sox became the lone concern of his professional life (and, we might assume, the inescapable preoccupation of his personal moments as well).

With it, he was handed a job description that included two remarkably difficult and seemingly opposed tasks. One, to build up the scouting and player development groundwork of the organization to a point where it may consistently produce talented young players, while structuring all current trades and contracts to benefit the further expansion and retention of said young talent. This is an immensely complicated and painstakingly arduous task that requires constant input and consistent monitoring on the level of a major, multinational corporation. This then, was job one, the easy one.

Job two was more difficult. The task, quite simply: to put a Red Sox club capable of winning the World Series on the field—right now.

Even getting past the tremendous amount of work involved in either of these jobs, the two tasks seem opposed to one another on a simple, theoretical level. What helps one so clearly seems to hurt the other—the two do not seem compatible within the same organization. How can a team successfully build a talented farm system without negatively impacting the chances of its current, present success? Conversely, how can a team expend the resources and talent to build a team capable of winning *now* without negatively impacting its future, long-term success?

These are the questions posed to all general managers in all sports, and although many claim to pursue solutions to both, in practice most are forced to choose (and most, regrettably, choose this year over next decade), conceding that this opposition is too stark to reconcile and the two tasks really are, in the end, incompatible. It takes considerable intelligence to look at such irreconcilable problems and seek out a solution that meets both—it is problem-solving on a fairly lofty plane.

Fortunately for the Red Sox organization, Theo Epstein just happens to be a young man of considerable intelligence. He has been able, over his first two years, to realize that the answers to these two problems are not, in fact, mutually exclusive—they are simply difficult to find—and he and the talented group of minds surrounding him have worked toward finding these types of solutions. They have, in the end, worked toward building two futures at once, one immediate, the other distant. And so as Theo Epstein fields the last of his questions before Game Four of the ALCS, he finds himself in an odd, uncomfortable position, with the immediate future of his club compressed down into one baseball game, the result of which could bring the distant, long-term future of the Red Sox organization crashing into the present in only a few cool autumn hours. His answers have deflected this realization, have turned the conversation back on itself. The man whose only concern is the future now finds himself inescapably faced with the present.

## A People with a Past

Of course, aside from both future and present, there exists the one aspect of time that Epstein can never concern himself with, which also happens to be the one aspect many millions of Red Sox fans cannot help but concern themselves with—the past. Recent past, distant past, ancient past, it hardly matters; as Sox fans, we find time for it all. Easily. Last night's game leads us rather seamlessly to the previous week, which then coasts us back into the summer and a previous series, then it is only a quick step back to last October. From there, we easily fall back a decade, stumble over a few more Octobers, and we're off. Suddenly, within but a few moments of mentioning a single pitch from last night's game, we have covered our entire lives as Red Sox fans, and perhaps even the entire lives of several preceding generations.

As we trace through these wanderings, we find that the various threads of the past are not so incompatible with their counterparts in the future. We fans find it endlessly, almost effortlessly possible to connect moments and situations and answers to questions both in the immediate past and the dusty, distant reaches of history. A home run the previous night is made relevant to both through a series of simple deductions, connected in time and in the minds of fans to a home run a decade earlier, the player who hit it tied in neatly with a player a half-century gone, and the trade that brought him to this game part of the rippling effects of a trade made a long, long time ago.

Not all Red Sox fans make these casual connections, but many (perhaps most) do, if for no other reason than because the nature of Red Sox history has made them so apparent, so obvious. Among other fans of other teams, the past is a divided, segmented entity, sectioned off in the history books and in the minds of fans by the time between one championship and another (for Angels fans, there are two segments of the past, one before and one after 2002; for Cardinals fans, there is the block of past between 1946 and 1964/67, followed by '67 to '82, then '82 to the present; and so on).

Not so for Sox fans, in whose minds the past has stretched out in one smooth, unbroken sheet stretching deep into baseball antiquity. The connections we make when we think about last night's Sox game find no obstacles, no segments to hurdle as they glide back through the seasons and decades, no moments at which one period of Sox history stops abruptly and a new era begins. Instead, these connections seem to link one upon another—Manny to Yaz, Yaz to Ted—until every Sox team becomes one Sox team, every Sox season the same Sox season, every Sox game turned into every Sox game ever played.

# A Team in the Present

And this, in the end, brings us back to October 17, 2004, and the hours leading up to Game Four of the ALCS. Unlike Theo Epstein, for whom it is the specter of the future that threatens to crash in on his present, Sox fans at this moment feel a pressure knocking from the opposite direction—the past. It is the call of this smooth, unbroken past that presses down on the tense faces and tight, wringing hands that settle into Fenway for Game Four as another season (another number) seems imminently prepared to take its place alongside a long, consistent history.

For Epstein, it is the future of Red Sox baseball that he so uncomfortably holds at a distance as he makes his way from the pressroom. For the fans, it is the past. But between us there is, at this moment, still a bit of present (still a bit of baseball) to be dealt with, and both Theo Epstein, architect of the Red Sox' future, and the Red Sox fans around the world who act as caretakers of its past, settle in to look down upon Fenway Park and hold onto the present, even if it lasts no more than nine all-too-brief innings longer.

The present lasts for ten days. For ten days, both Theo Epstein and Sox fans everywhere sit (and stand and jump up and down and enjoy) eighty innings, over which no shadow of the future is cast, and from which no burdens of the past hang. Instead, for eight games over ten days, there is only present, and nothing else. And at the very end of these ten days of present, Theo Epstein once again faces a reporter—only this time, he is standing; this time he is wearing a soaked T-shirt over his suit; this time he is holding a chilled bottle of champagne in his hand; and, this time, he is smiling.

He stands on the championship platform in the visitors' clubhouse in St. Louis, and although the ten days of present are not quite over, the reporter who leans a microphone toward him immediately tries to pull the past back into the room. She asks if he ever thought, back when the Sox were down 3-0 in the ALCS, that this moment would be possible. Without hesitation, Epstein answers with one quick word, *No*, then smiles wide and runs a hand back through his champagne-drenched hair. No, he did not, and no, most of us did not either; but then it happened nonetheless.

Somewhere between a general manager obsessed with the future and fans obsessed with the past was a team obsessed with neither—a team only concerned with the present. And through it, through ten days of no past and no future, of only the present team playing the present game, history was made. A break, between past and future, and in the ten days between, only present.

But then the reporter next to Theo does not seem to understand this (not quite), as her next question tries to pull the future beyond this line and into the present. She asks about next season, about the impending free agents, and so on. Theo cuts her off before she can finish, shakes his head, and speaks for himself and for all Sox fans when he says, *That's a question for another night*, then takes a long pull of champagne and laughs through a wide smile. It is, of course, a question for the future. And Theo, the Sox fan who grew up in Brookline, understands that on this night of all nights, the future can wait. Like all Sox fans who have suffered through and with the past, he asks only to be allowed to enjoy this present a bit longer.

As do we all, fans and players and executives alike, who in the late hours of October 27, 2004, ask only to enjoy this moment a bit longer . . . to have a few more sips of champagne and give one more high-five and one more hug; to call one more fan and friend across the country; to linger a bit; to watch Manny reach his destination and see Wake holding the golden trophy; to see Pedro and Schilling (our two aces) celebrate together; to watch Tek and D-Lowe (who came here together) celebrate as teammates and champions; to spend a few more moments among the faces and character and charisma of these players, of these Red Sox, just a few moments longer, before the night ends and the champagne dries . . . before this team parts and continues on into the future, and leaves this present—and they, too, become part of history.

**Idiot Rule:** *The future can wait.*

# Acknowledgments

The road this book traveled to completion was neither as long nor as difficult as that of the 2004 Boston Red Sox; but, like the Sox, it too was a collaborative effort. Among those whose contributions proved invaluable along this road, and whose names deserve mention under its cover, are Jaimie Muehlhausen, designer and co-founder of Bartlett Park; Trisha Saintelus, John O'Rourke, and Jerry Remy at *The Remy Report*; Paula Munier and Laura MacLaughlin at Adams Media; and, in particular, Mr. Larry Kay, who for myself and for this book was the scout in the bleachers who looked in, saw something, and made a call.

# Index